KnOCK 'em DEaD

SECRETS & STRATEGIES
— FOR SUCCESS IN AN —
UNCERTAIN WORLD

How to Take Control of
Your Job Search, Career, and Life!

The latest from *New York Times* bestseller

MARTIN YATE, CPC

AVON, MASSACHUSETTS

Acknowledgments

I would like to thank the following people for their help in helping bring *Secrets & Strategies* to life: Peter Archer and Karen Cooper at Adams Media for inviting me to do the book and weathering the tornadoes that accompanied its gestation and birth. William Yate for his exceptional copyediting and editorial direction on a project with almost impossible deadlines. And my friends and colleagues who served on the book's Expert Panel and whose comments added another dimension to the work. It was wonderful to work with these brilliant people again. Especially Bob Morris, the headhunter who thirty years ago recruited me for the most important job change of my career, and Marjean, Glenna, Maynard, Rick, Al, and Bill, whom I met and worked with as a result; and Bootsie for being such a special and unique human being.

Published by
Adams Media, a division of F+W Media, Inc.
57 Littlefield Street, Avon, MA 02322. U.S.A.
www.adamsmedia.com

Trade Paperback Edition	Knock 'Em Dead Job Search Kit Edition
ISBN 10: 1-4405-0650-7	ISBN 10: 1-4405-2837-3
ISBN 13: 978-1-4405-0650-5	ISBN 13: 978-1-4405-2837-8
eISBN 10: 1-4405-1201-9	
eISBN 13: 978-1-4405-1201-8	

Printed in the United States of America.

10 9 8 7 6 5 4 3 2 1

Library of Congress Cataloging-in-Publication Data
is available from the publisher.

This publication is designed to provide accurate and authoritative information with regard to the subject matter covered. It is sold with the understanding that the publisher is not engaged in rendering legal, accounting, or other professional advice. If legal advice or other expert assistance is required, the services of a competent professional person should be sought.
—From a *Declaration of Principles* jointly adopted by a Committee of the American Bar Association and a Committee of Publishers and Associations

Many of the designations used by manufacturers and sellers to distinguish their product are claimed as trademarks. Where those designations appear in this book and Adams Media was aware of a trademark claim, the designations have been printed with initial capital letters.

This book is available at quantity discounts for bulk purchases.
For information, please call 1-800-289-0963.

Praise for *Knock 'em Dead: The Ultimate Job Search Guide*

"Classic winner. . . . A bestseller for two decades, this is one of the most valuable career books on the market."

—*L.A. Times*

"The best book on job hunting."

—*Financial Times*

"Some great advice can be found in Martin Yate's *Knock 'em Dead.*"

—*USA Today*

"Comprehensive, fast-paced, upbeat style."

—*BusinessWeek*

"Classic. . . ."

—*U.S. News and World Report*

"The first, middle, and last word for job seekers on navigating a competitive, and often cutthroat, job market."

—*Science Daily*

"If Martin Yate writes it, I'm going to recommend it. He's really just about the best in the business when it comes to providing clear, effective, and reasonable job search processes."

—*ALL Business, a Dunn & Bradstreet company*

"Should be required reading for job hunters."

—*Library Journal*

"5 stars out of 5 stars."

—*Las Vegas Review-Journal*

CONTENTS

This Is Your Life ix

The Panel of Experts xv

CHAPTER 1
Wake Up, Stand Up, Lively Up Your Life 1
How business works, why jobs exist, and what this means to you.

CHAPTER 2
We Are All Professional Schizophrenics 7
We all develop a new, valid, and separate persona when we enter
the professional world. Your dedication to the development of this
professional self, and the transferable skills and professional values that
underlie it, will determine the trajectory and success of your career.

CHAPTER 3
Your Resume Has to Be a Killer for You to Survive 21
Your resume is the most important financial document you will ever
own. When it works, you do, but when it doesn't work, you don't either.

CHAPTER 4

The Network-Integrated Plan of Attack 41

A successful job search depends on what you know *and* who you know. Learn how recruitment works, and how to integrate networking into every job search strategy.

CHAPTER 5

How to Build Networks for Today and Tomorrow 46

How to build deep, resilient, and relevant networks for this job search and the next one.

CHAPTER 6

Job Sites, Resume Banks, Headhunters, and Direct Research 59

How to leverage each of these strategies and build networking tactics into each of them. Learn how to quadruple your chances of an interview with any job opening.

CHAPTER 7

Reach Out and Touch Someone 67

Little happens in the professional world without conversations taking place. How to get into conversations as quickly and as often as possible with the people who have the power to hire you.

CHAPTER 8

Prepare to Win 86

Learn the preparation strategies that set the stage for turning job interviews into job offers.

CHAPTER 9

The Five Secrets of the Hire 97

There are five secrets behind any hire that has ever been made.

CHAPTER 10

Meet Your Interviewers:
Why They Do the Things They Do..................103

How do interviewers organize interviews? How do they think, and why do they ask the questions they do?

CHAPTER 11

Knock 'em Dead at the Interview 115

How to handle some of the toughest, most frequently asked job interview questions.

CHAPTER 12

Out of Sight Can Mean Out of Mind.................143

Follow-up tactics to maintain your visibility and advance your candidacy.

CHAPTER 13

Job Offer Negotiations 152

How to negotiate money, benefits, and the employment contract; plus questions to help you evaluate the opportunity.

CHAPTER 14

Starting on the Right Foot 165

How to establish a foundation for future success in the first ninety days.

CHAPTER 15

Climbing the Ladder of Success 170

How to secure your job, pursue and land promotions, and gain access to the inner circle, where your job is safest and where the plum assignments and promotions live.

CHAPTER 16

Lifetime Career Management—Issues and Strategies 181

How to achieve a more secure and meaningful life. A new way to look at career choice, career change, and the pursuit of your dreams.

APPENDIX

The Expert Database. 203

Professional, biographical, and contact information for each member of the panel of experts.

Index. 218

THIS IS YOUR LIFE

Let me tell you a little bit about yourself.

You didn't come to this book for a good time; you came because you need to make changes. You need to get back to work, out of a dead-end job, or perhaps you simply think there must be a better way to make a success of your professional life. *You came to this book today because you decided to change your life for the better.*

Let me tell you something else I know:

- You are somewhere along the path of what will likely be a fifty-year work life.
- During this time you can expect economic recessions to swing by every 7–10 years.
- You will change jobs (not always by choice) about every four years.
- You will probably have three or more distinct careers over the span of your professional life.

These job changes, coming round approximately every four years, add up to twelve or more job changes over fifty years, with three of them involving the much greater challenges and financial dislocation associated with changing, not just your job, but your entire career.

You know it is time for a radical shift in your career management strategy because you realize that the advice you've been given— choose one thing you like and stick to it for the next fifty years; get an education, choose a career, settle down to it, and do a good job; patience and loyalty will be rewarded with job security and life success—doesn't make sense in today's uncertain and rapidly changing world. We live in a world where greed has turned your life into a disposable commodity that will be used and discarded, unless you *take control and change the trajectory of your life.* And if you hope to achieve consistent professional success and financial stability in this world, you *must* take control.

The first step is to face the facts of professional life in the twenty-first century:

Change is constant; it is a given in your professional world. A successful career is no longer a given; it doesn't come as a gift with the purchase of your college diploma. It's a critical aspect of your life and it needs management. You must adapt to the realities of a professional world where there is no certainty, but perhaps more opportunity. With continual rapid change becoming a constant in our lives, those who learn to live with uncertainty and who can adapt to the needs of an ever-changing professional landscape are perfectly positioned to seize the abundant opportunities that always accompany a changing of the eras. Recognize that change is constant; grasp the fact that, by taking responsibility for your destiny and continuing to adapt and evolve, you can change your situation today, and your tomorrows forever.

Job search and career management skills are the most important skills you can ever develop. Companies today have no sense of loyalty to their employees; they have loyalty to the shareholders, and the shareholders are only concerned with profit *now*, this quarter. You are a cog in the moneymaking machine, and if an employer can find a way to make money, or save money by automating or exporting your job, then your head will be on the chopping block. That's the way things are, so cast off any mistaken notions of thick-and-thin fidelity to your employer and focus your attention with laser-like precision on you: What's best for *your* career and for *your* life?

Consider yourself your own corporation, make it a mantra. It's easier to evaluate your strengths, to see where weaknesses need fixing, to set plans for where the corporation (you) is going.

Marjean Bean, CPC. President, Medit Staff. Information technology. 30+ years' experience.

Enlightened Self-Interest

When a company dispenses with your services, it's nothing personal: The company is doing what it must do to survive and satisfy the shareholders. You need to do the same thing: Take control of your life, your economic survival, and your success by acting with the same forethought, objectivity, and self-interest as a corporation.

Let's take that a step further: Start thinking of yourself as a company—as MeInc, a financial entity that must survive and prosper over the long haul. *You are MeInc,* a brand new start-up with a successful future to be won.

As MeInc, you have products and services to sell: the skills and experience you've accumulated over the course of your working life. *These product and services have to fulfill the needs of your customers, or the sale will go to a competitor.*

This means that MeInc needs to organize and structure its activities. You will need:

- *Research and Development:* to identify and develop products with the maximum marketplace appeal. In other words, you have to monitor market demands and develop the skills employers need, not just now but continually.
- *Marketing and Public Relations:* to establish credibility for the professional services you deliver, and to ensure that this credibility becomes visible to an ever-widening circle, starting with your current department and expanding outwards through the company, your local professional community, and beyond, as your strategic career plans dictate.

- *Sales:* to constantly develop new strategies to sell your products and services, including resume, job search, interviewing, negotiation, and other career management tools.

- *Strategic Planning:* to plan strategies for growth within the company, time strategic career moves that take you to new employers, monitor the health of your profession, and make plans for career change; and all *on your timetable.* Working with R & D and Marketing, Strategic Planning will also constantly monitor opportunities and strategies for the pursuit of completely new revenue streams—alternate entrepreneurial endeavors that minimize disruption of MeInc's cash flow and maximize the odds of success for these endeavors.

- *Finance:* to ensure you invest wisely in initiatives that will deliver a Return On Investment. You must invest in your future, in your success, rather than fritter away your income on the instant gratification drummed into your head by 24/7 media. This is important: You have been raised to be a good consumer and to live in debt. You probably spend eight hours a day in front of a screen and absorb around 3,000 advertising messages a day. To make your dreams come true, you have to break free of this indoctrination and invest yourself, your time, and your income in the activities that will make MeInc successful and give you the opportunity for a fulfilling life.

How should I manage my life/my career differently? Manage your life as if you are your own boss and agent.

Mike Squires, Senior Technical Recruiter, PayPal, an eBay Company. 15 years' experience.

If the idea of taking a more businesslike approach to your career makes sense, *Knock 'em Dead: Secrets & Strategies* will give you the tools to make it happen. I've been at this for more than thirty years; it's what I think about every day. Over this time, in fourteen books, countless articles, blogs, presentations, workshops, and webinars I have developed a practical, commonsense approach to achieving success in your professional life. It's an approach that weaves resume, job search, interview, career choice, career change, entrepreneurial endeavor, and the many other issues that affect lifetime career management into a single cohesive approach to survival and success; and I include "survival" mindfully, because when you think in terms of a half-century work life—it ain't no sprint, babycakes.

> **View career management as a life-long process** and job loss will become much less frequent and much less traumatic when it does occur.
>
> Faith Sheaffer-Polen, Senior Career Coach, CareerCurve. Organizational psychology. 15 years' experience.

The problem is that to absorb all this knowledge, up until now you would have had to read my fourteen books, as well as all my articles and blogs, and attended many of those workshops and webinars, because this approach has evolved over the many years I have spent thinking, writing, and talking about these issues.

Knock 'em Dead: Secrets & Strategies brings all these diverse threads together in a single narrative, giving you the *must-have* knowledge and tools to get your career and your life back on the right track and keep them there.

I didn't set out in life to become a career management expert; just as your ultimate career path may not be the one you initially chose, neither was mine. My career and expertise evolved as a result of other jobs giving me an unusually comprehensive understanding of the world of work, and these professional experiences combined with an ability to communicate, an inquiring mind, and a passion for helping others. The result is that almost thirty-five years later I have thought through these job search, career management, and success issues very carefully. It isn't ivory tower theory either: I've been in the trenches as an international technology headhunter, a Director of HR for a publicly traded technology company, and a Director of Training and Development for a division of a *Fortune* 500 company. In these capacities I have been at the table for countless hires, promotions, and terminations.

Knock 'em Dead: Secrets & Strategies is going to be a conversation in which I talk to you about the issues that are crucial to getting out of this tough spot in your life and into a better place for the future, so that you understand how integrated job search and career management work and how to play the game to win.

> **Bosses are less and less able** to make promises to their workers about tenure of employment, even if they want to.
>
> Dr. Jim Bright, Partner, Bright & Associates, Australia. Author, *Chaos Theory of Careers*. 22 years' experience.

Along the path of my career, I've met thousands of professionals in fields related to employment, and I've chosen a select group of forty-two resume writers, headhunters, corporate recruiters, HR professionals, and career management experts to join us; and as you have already begun to see, they will be adding another dimension to our dialogue.

Choosing the quotes I use to enrich the conversation you and I are beginning was difficult because they had so many good things to say and I only have so many pages; and it occurred to me that you might like to see their full commentary on some sixty job search and career management issues I address in the book. So on the Career Advice pages at *www.knockemdead.com* you'll find a tab for *Secrets & Strategies*, and there you will be able to access the full wisdom of my friends and colleagues.

What you hold in your hands are the essentials for building a successful professional life, and you'll see my esteemed professional colleagues adding to the conversation in very perceptive ways. If you hope to achieve consistent professional success and the financial stability that accompanies it, I have a plan and we're here to help.

—*Martin Yate, CPC*

The Panel of Experts

I'd like to introduce you to my panel of experts: forty-two extremely savvy career management professionals. They bring expertise in a wide range of professional disciplines and hail from all over the United States and from as far away as the United Kingdom and Australia. I've known a few of them for thirty years or more, and we've worked, played, and argued together about the issues in this book for years. There are only three things they hold in common: They know what they're talking about, they don't pussyfoot around, and they each genuinely care. Meet the gang:

Wendy Adams, Founder, The Career Coach. Transitions. 20 years' experience.

Nancy C. Anton, CPC. Talent Consultant, CIGNA. 20 years' experience.

Marjean Bean, CPC. President, Medit Staff. Information technology. 30+ years' experience.

Alesia Benedict, CPRW, JCTC. CEO, GetInterviews.com. Resumes, social media. 20+ years' experience.

Jay Block, President, The Jay Block Companies. Employment and workplace strategist. Author, *The Proteus Solution*. 20+ years' experience.

Dr. Jim Bright, Partner, Bright & Associates, Australia. Author, *Chaos Theory of Careers*. 22 years' experience.

Glenna Cose Brin, CPC. President, AllianceStaff. High-end administration. 30+ years' experience.

Joe Camarada, President, CAM Search and Consulting. HR and Finance search. 25 years' experience.

Paul Cameron, President, DriveStaff Inc. Technology recruitment. 14 years' experience.

Maynard G. Charron, President, Paper Industry Recruitment. 30+ years' experience.

Lisa Chenofsky Singer, Chenofsky Singer and Associates. Communications and Human Resources Consulting. 20+ years' experience.

Allison Farber Cheston, Career Advisor, Allison Cheston & Associates. Author, *In the Driver's Seat: Work-Life Skills for Young Adults*. 28 years' experience.

Marsha Connolly, Managing Partner, The New River Group. Certified Executive Coach. 30 years' experience.

Grant Cooper, President, Careerpro of New Orleans. Strategic Resumes. 17 years' experience.

Al Daum, CPC. Alan N. Daum & Associates. Process automation engineering. 36 years' experience.

Rich Gold, CPC. Senior Recruiter, Smith Arnold Partners. Finance recruiter. 20 years' experience.

Meg Guiseppi, C-level Executive Job Search Coach, Executive Career Brand. 20+ years' experience.

Michelle Hagans, Recruiter, Anu Resources Unlimited. IT and medical. 20+ years' experience.

Rick Kean, Consultant Emeritus, A. M. Hamilton, Inc. Staffing and training. 30+ years' experience.

Sean Koppelman, President, The Talent Magnet. Advertising, beauty, and entertainment. 16 years' experience.

Eric Kramer, Chief Innovation Officer, Innovative Career Services. Psychologist, career and interview coaching. 10 years' experience.

Janice Litvin, Executive Search Consultant, Micro Search. High-tech, marketing. 20 years' experience.

Rob Lockard, SPHR. HR Manager, The Centech Group. 9 years' experience.

Valentino Martinez, President, Martinez Group. Recruitment and University Relations. 38 years' experience.

Karen McGrath, PHR. Talent Acquisition Manager, Enterprise Rent-A-Car. 22 years' experience.

Jackie Mills, Office Angels, Birmingham, United Kingdom. Administration recruitment. 14 years' experience.

John Mooney, J. Mooney dba Consultive Source. 20+ years' experience.

Bob Morris, Owner, Storage Placements. Data storage sales/marketing. 44 years' experience.

Joe Murawski, CPC. Executive Search Consultant, Focused Hire. Aerospace, defense, and high-tech electronics. 15 years' experience.

Perry Newman, CPC/CSMS. Executive Resume Writer/Career Coach. 25 years' experience.

Olga Ocon, Executive Recruiter, Busch International. VP and CEO-level searches in high-tech. 15 years' experience.

George Olmstead, Managing Partner, Olmstead Lynch & Kreutz. Senior management recruitment. 30 years' experience.

Don Orlando, MBA, CPRW, JCTC. Owner, The McLean Group. Coaching senior executives. 17 years' experience.

Faith Sheaffer-Polen, Senior Career Coach, CareerCurve. Organizational psychology. 15 years' experience.

Jim Rohan, Senior Partner, J P Canon Associates. Supply chain management. 25 years' experience.

Nancy Schuman, CSP. Corporate VP Marketing, Lloyd Staffing. 30 years' experience.

Mike Squires, Senior Technical Recruiter, PayPal, an eBay Company. 15 years' experience.

Dean Swett, President, Paramour Group. Gaming and 3D graphics. 26 years' experience.

Bob Waldo, Principal Consultant, Best Hire Consulting Services. 20 years' experience.

Ron Weisinger, Principal Development, LINKS Consulting. Human Resources. 20 years' experience.

Bill Wilhelm, CPC. Executive Recruiter, Wilhelm and Associates, Inc. Industrial Sales and Manufacturing Management. 38 years' experience.

Denise Wilkerson, RN, CPC. Executive Search Director, Global Edge Recruiting. Medical devices, biotech, pharma, sales/marketing management. 14+ years' experience.

Christine Wunderlin, Christine Wunderlin Consulting. Career development. 14+ years' experience.

CHAPTER 1

WAKE UP, STAND UP,
LIVELY UP YOUR LIFE

You may have come to these pages fully employed and ready for that next step, or you may have been laid off. If the latter, your overwhelming emotion right now is probably panic. Your brain whispers, "Maybe this is it; maybe I'll never find another job; maybe my career is in ruins."

Some of this is a natural reaction to losing a job—grieving mixed with anger manifests itself as an anxiety crisis. It's understandable because today's world is completely different from five or ten years ago, and the pace of change is accelerating. Your panic also reflects the fact that, like most people, you probably hadn't planned for this: You had your sweet blond curls stuck in the sand.

If you are going to survive and prosper over the long haul, you have to pull your head out of the sand—or wherever else you had it stuck—and start getting actively involved in the management of your life. This is *your* life, and what you make of it is up to you, because no one else gives a damn. I'll show you how to get your professional life under control and onto the right track, and I'll give you many of the tools to do it, but bottom line: *It's your life, and what you make of it is up to you.*

There is no promise of a future reward unless you make it happen.

Rick Kean, Consultant Emeritus, A. M. Hamilton, Inc. Staffing and training. 30+ years' experience.

I'm going to share a plan with you that will help you achieve *a complete career management makeover* as you organize and execute your job search and get a fresh start with a good new job. You are going to learn a reasoned approach to building a killer resume; a plan of attack for your job search that integrates networking into every strategy; how to turn job interviews into job offers; and how to negotiate salary.

You will also learn how to get off on the right foot in your new job; how to make your job more secure and how to pursue and win promotions; how to plan and execute career changes on *your* timetable; and how to simultaneously pursue those alternate entrepreneurial and dream careers you barely dare dream about. You haven't read a book like this before, so relax and go with the program; I won't waste your time.

Think about Your Goals

What do I want out of life? The more clearly you can envision life goals, including those dreams everyone told you not to waste your time with, and see a real path to achieving some of them, the more effort you will put into the work that has to be done today and every day along the path that brings them to reality.

Evaluate your career to date. Be honest with yourself about where you stand today and why. It isn't someone else's fault—like it or not, you are largely responsible for where you are. Honestly accepting this is the first step along a path that takes you to greater financial security and professional success. What should you have done differently? What can you learn from your mistakes so that you can move forward, rather than live condemned to repeating them?

Now look at where you want to be ten or twenty years from now. And those interests and dreams that give meaning to your life? Stop cramming them under the bed: Haul them out and re-examine them as you read and learn—you might find they don't belong there. Bring all these long-term goals and dreams into focus; own them, don't be scared by what others might think and don't give up before you've started.

This is not an either/or world. You *can* have multiple career goals and multiple career paths: for climbing the corporate ladder, for starting your own business, for writing that book or becoming a painter; other people have made it happen, and you can too. But like many others, you have been told: "Find *one* thing you like, make it your career and settle down to it for a lifetime." But most of what you have been told doesn't make sense; life isn't that simple and you are too complex a being. I like to write; but all day, every day for fifty years? *Sweet baby Jesus, I'm ready, take me now.*

> **Broaden the sources of your income.** Do not rely on one source of income but rather a portfolio of options.
>
> Lisa Chenofsky Singer, Chenofsky Singer and Associates. Communications and Human Resources Consulting. 20+ years' experience.

You might have dreams for career paths that seem impossible or that common sense tells you are hare-brained; yet all of them hold value and could well be achievable. Whatever those dreams might be, they are going to fall into one of three categories:

1. *Core career:* I'll show you how best to land that next job and how to make it as secure as it can possibly be; how to land the plum assignments, win raises and promotions; how to navigate strategic career moves within your industry; even how to decide on new career paths including when and how to make the migration and become successful in your new field.
2. *Dream career:* Your dream might be to become a writer, painter, singer in the band, or a landscape gardener. I'll show you the key strategies that can bring your dreams to life.
3. *Entrepreneurial career:* You'll learn how to seamlessly integrate plans for an entrepreneurial career into the continuing pursuit of success in your *core career.* You'll recognize that they aren't mutually exclusive: They are attainable and can even be complementary.

We'll develop the means for achieving them throughout the book and bring them together in Chapter 16. But don't jump ahead: There's a plan, a methodology, and a new way of looking at your professional life that you need to soak up before it will all make sense and enable you to pursue *multiple parallel career paths.*

> **Understand the rules of the workplace as they are today.** Stay one step ahead instead of two steps behind the changes.
>
> Perry Newman, CPC/CSMS. Executive Resume Writer/Career Coach. 25 years' experience.

Start Toward Your Goals *Now*

Your successful career is a marathon, not a sprint, so whatever your goals, the sooner you start toward them the better. Start imagining what you want your life to be like, not just for this job search and that next job, but a detailed picture of what a fulfilling life would look like for you.

With achievable goals, you will be re-energized and your life will be enriched by their pursuit, knowing you have a real chance of making them come true. Every day, when you wake up on the right side of the grass you are ahead of the game: You are alive, and you have a plan to make your dreams come true, one that takes you step-by-step from where you stand today to where you want to stand tomorrow.

All these things are possible, but it starts with getting your priorities straight, and your priority right now is getting back to work or out of that hell-hole cubicle in the high-rise salt mine that you inhabit today.

A long time ago, President Calvin Coolidge said, "The business of America is business." You might not agree, but it's certainly true that business is at the heart of American prosperity. Even in times when unemployment has soared and banks have crumbled, across the country the wheels continue to turn, stuff continues to get made, and people continue to get jobs.

Even during an economic downturn—remember, they're cyclical and will occur regularly throughout your work life—there are jobs. We have a huge economy; there are *always* jobs. Even in the worst months of the current recession, at least *four million new jobs* were posted every month on Internet job sites. But companies won't always show up on your doorstep, begging you to accept generous offers. Finding a job and advancing your career is *work*. It takes concentrated effort, and begins with understanding why jobs exist.

How Business Works

Companies exist to make money for the owners, as quickly, efficiently, and reliably as possible. They make money by selling a product or service, and they prosper by becoming better and more efficient at it. When a company saves time, it saves money, and then has more time to make more money; this is called productivity.

If a company can make money without employees, it will do so, because that means more money for the owners. Unfortunately for the owners, a company requires a complex machinery to deliver those products and services that bring in revenue. Every job is a small but important cog in this complex moneymaking machine, and every cog has to be oiled and maintained. That costs money. If the company can redesign the machinery to do without that cog (automation) or can find a cheaper cog (outsourcing that job to Mumbai), of course it is going to do so.

> **You are responsible for your own job security.** Watch for the "writing on the wall" at work, for signs of reorganizations or downsizing.
>
> Christine Wunderlin, aka Coach Christine on the *Career Czar*. Wunderlin Consulting. 30+ years' experience.

There are two reasons job exist. First, as I've said, every job is a small but important cog in the corporation's complex moneymaking machine. Second, the company hasn't been able to automate that job out of existence because in your area of technical expertise, problems arise.

Consequently, the company hires someone who has the *technical skills* to solve these problems when they occur and who knows the territory well enough to predict and prevent many of these problems from arising in the first place. It doesn't matter what your job title is, you are always hired to be a problem-solver with a specific area of expertise.

Think about the nuts and bolts of a job you've held. Whatever the job, it always comes down to *anticipating, preventing, and solving problems*. This enables the company to make money for the owners as quickly, efficiently, and reliably as possible.

These aren't the only factors that are critical to your success and that all jobs have in common. In the next chapter you'll learn about a specific set of *transferable skills* and *professional values* that all employers are anxious to find in candidates, whom they then hire just as quickly as they can find them. The skills and values that you'll learn in this book have applications far beyond your core career.

CHAPTER 2

WE ARE ALL PROFESSIONAL
SCHIZOPHRENICS

Over the years I've read a lot of books about finding jobs, winning promotions, and managing your career. A few were insightful and many were innocuous, but one theme that runs through them all is plain harmful: Just be yourself.

"Who you are is just fine. Be yourself and you'll do fine." Wrong. Remember that first day on your first job, when you went to get your first cup of coffee? You found the coffee machine, and there, stuck on the wall behind it, was a handwritten sign reading:

YOUR MOTHER DOESN'T WORK HERE
PICK UP AFTER YOURSELF

You thought, "Pick up after myself? Gee, that means I can't behave like I do at home and get away with it." And so you started to observe and emulate the more successful professionals around you. You behaved in a way that was appropriate to the environment, and in doing so demonstrated *emotional intelligence*. Over time you developed many new ways of conducting yourself at work in order to be accepted as a professional in your field. You weren't born this way. You developed a behavioral profile, a *professional persona* that enabled you to survive in the professional world.

> **:ess?** Turn off the TV—and invest in improving your value
> to the marketplace. You can't afford to go to bed as stupid as
> you woke up. If you do not learn something new every day to
> become more valuable to the marketplace tomorrow, you will
> become worth less (worthless).
>
> Jay Block, President, The Jay Block Companies. Employment and workplace
> strategist. Author, *The Proteus Solution*. 20+ years' experience.

Some people are just better than the average bear at everything they do, and they become more successful as a result. It doesn't happen by accident, there is a specific set of *transferable skills* and *professional values* that underlies professional success: skills and values that employers all over the world in every industry and profession are anxious to find in candidates from the entry-level to the boardroom. Why this isn't taught in schools and in the university programs that cost a small fortune is unfathomable, because these skills and values are the foundation of every successful career. They break down into these groups:

1. *The Technical Skills of Your Current Profession.* These are the technical competencies that give you the *ability* to do your job and the know-how to use your skills productively and efficiently. These *technical skills* are mandatory if you want to land a job within your profession. *Technical skills,* while transferable, vary from profession to profession, so many of your current *technical skills* will only be transferable within your current profession.
2. *Transferable Skills That Apply in All Professions.* The set of skills that underlies your ability to execute the *technical skills* of your job effectively, whatever your job might be. They are the foundation of all the professional success you will experience in this and any other career (including dream and entrepreneurial careers) that you may pursue over the years.

> **Transferable skills** are the most important element to thriving
> with job changes.
>
> Nancy C. Anton, CPC. Talent Consultant, CIGNA. 20 years' experience.

3. *Professional Values.* A set of beliefs that enable all professionals to make the many judgment calls required during the working day to ensure the best interests of the department and the employer are always promoted. They complement the *transferable skills* and together form a firm foundation for a successful professional life.

> **How important are *transferable skills?*** Absolutely critical. Many candidates are "qualified" in that they possess the technical skills for the job. Transferable skills go to how well they apply that technical knowledge.
>
> Ron Weisinger, Principal Development, LINKS Consulting. Human Resources. 20 years' experience.

A Review of Transferable Skills and Professional Values

As you read through the following breakdown of each *transferable skill* and *professional value* you may, for example, read about *communication*, and think, "Yes, I can see how communication skills are important in all jobs and at all levels of the promotional ladder, and, hallelujah, I have good communication skills." Take time to recall examples of your *communication skills* and the role they play in the success of your work.

You might also read about *multitasking skills* and realize that here is something that needs more work. Whenever you identify a *transferable skill* that needs work, you have found a *professional development project* that will repay your attention for the rest of your working life, no matter how you make a living.

Here are the *transferable skills* and *professional values* that will speed the conclusion of this job search and your long-term professional success. You'll find that you already have some of them to a greater or lesser degree, and if you are committed to making a success of your life, you'll commit to further development of all of them.

le Skills	▶ Professional Values
..al	Motivation and Energy
Critical Thinking	Commitment and Reliability
Communication	Determination
Multitasking	Pride and Integrity
Teamwork	Productivity
Leadership	Systems and Procedures
Creativity	

▶ Transferable Skills

TECHNICAL SKILLS

The *technical skills* of your job are the foundation of success within your current profession; without them you won't even land a job, much less keep it for long or win a promotion. They speak to your *ability* to do the job, those essential skills necessary for the day-to-day execution of your duties. These *technical skills* vary from profession to profession and do not refer to anything technical *as such* or to technology.

However, it is a given that one of the *technical skills* essential to every job is technological competence. You must be proficient in all the technology and Internet-based applications relevant to your work. Even when you are not working in a technology field, strong *technology skills* will enhance your stability and help you leverage professional growth.

Some of your technology skills will only be relevant within your current profession, while others (Word, Excel, PowerPoint, to name the obvious) will be transferable across all industry and professional lines. Staying current with the *technical* and *technology skills* of your chosen career path is the keystone of your professional stability and growth.

CRITICAL THINKING SKILLS

As I noted in the last chapter, your job, whatever it is, exists to solve problems and to prevent problems from arising within your area of expertise. *Critical thinking, analytical,* or *problem-solving skills* represent a systematic approach to dealing with the challenges presented by your work. *Critical thinking skills* allow you to think through a problem, define the challenge and its possible solutions, and then evaluate and implement the best solution from all available options.

> **Transferable skills?** Critical. For example, assuming two candidates with equal technical skills for the job, the one who really has critical thinking skills is leaps and bounds ahead.
>
> Marjean Bean, CPC. President, Medit Staff. Information technology. 30+ years' experience.

Fifty percent of the success of any project is in the preparation, *critical thinking* is at the heart of that preparation, and a properly defined problem always leads to a better solution.

COMMUNICATION SKILLS

Every professional job today demands good *communication skills*, but what are they? All the transferable skills are interconnected—for example, good *verbal skills* require both *listening* and *critical thinking skills* to accurately process incoming information and enable you to present your outgoing verbal messaging persuasively in light of the interests and sophistication of your audience so that it is understood and accepted.

When the professional world talks about *communication skills*, it is referring, not just to listening and speaking, but to four primary skills and four supportive skills.

The primary *communication skills* are:

- *Verbal skills*—what you say and how you say it.
- *Listening skills*—listening to understand, rather than just waiting your turn to talk.
- *Writing skills*—clear written communication creates a lasting impression of who you are and is essential for success in any professional career.
- *Technology communication skills*—your ability to eva' tocols, strengths, and weaknesses of alternative c' media, and then to choose the medium appropriate' and message.

The four supportive *communication skills* are:

- *Grooming and dress*—these tell others who you are and how you feel about yourself.
- *Social graces*—how you behave toward others in all situations; this defines your professionalism.
- *Body language*—this displays how you're feeling deep inside, a form of communication that predates speech. For truly effective communication, what your mouth says must be in harmony with what your body says.
- *Emotional IQ*—your emotional self-awareness, your maturity in dealing with others in the full range of human interactions.

Develop effective skills in all eight of the subsets that together comprise *communication skills* and you'll gain enormous control over what you can achieve, how you are perceived, and what happens in your life.

MULTITASKING

Multitasking. I can't think of a single professional job that does not require the ability to multitask.

Michelle Hagans, Recruiter, Anu Resources Unlimited. IT and medical. 20+ years' experience.

This is one of the most desirable skills of the new era. According to numerous studies, however, the *multitasking* demands of modern professional life are causing massive frustration and meltdowns for professionals everywhere. The problem is NOT *multitasking*, the problem is the assumption that *multitasking* means being reactive to *all* incoming stimuli and therefore jumping around from one task to another as the emergency of the moment dictates. Such a definition of *multitasking* would of course leave you feeling that wild horses are attached to your extremities and tearing you limb from limb.

Few people understand what *multitasking* abilities are built on: *time management* and *organizational* abilities. Here are the basics.

Establish Priorities:
Multitasking is based on three things:

1. Being organized
2. Establishing priorities
3. Managing your time

The Plan, Do, Review Cycle:
At the end of every day you review the day:

- What happened: A.M. and P.M.?
- What went well? Do more of it.
- What went wrong? How do you fix it?
- What projects do I need to move forward tomorrow?
- Rank each project. A= must be completed tomorrow. B= Good to be completed tomorrow. C= if there is spare time from A and B priorities.
- Make a prioritized To Do list.
- Stick to it.

Doing this at the end of the day keeps you informed about what you have achieved, and lets you know that you have invested your time in the most important activities today and will tomorrow, so you feel better, sleep better, and come in the next day focused and ready to rock.

TEAMWORK

Companies depend on teams because the professional world revolves around the complex challenges of making money, and such complexities require teams of people to provide ongoing solutions. This means that you must work efficiently and respectfully with other people who have totally different responsibilities, backgrounds, objectives, and areas of expertise. It's true that individual initiative is important, but as a professional much of the really important work you do will be done as a member of a group. Your long-term stability and success require that you learn the arts of cooperation, team-based decision-making, and team communication.

Teamwork demands that a commitment to the team and its success comes first. This means you take on a task because it needs to be done, not because it makes you look good.

As a team player you:

- Always cooperate.
- Always make decisions based on team goals.
- Always keep team members informed.
- Always keep commitments.
- Always share credit, never blame.

If you become a successful leader in your professional life, it's a given that you were first a reliable team player, because a leader must understand the dynamics of teamwork before she can leverage them. When teamwork is coupled with the other *transferable skills* and *professional values, it results in greater responsibility and promotions.*

> **Teamwork.** It's a cliché but it's true and wise to remember . . .
> that there is no I in T-E-A-M.
>
> Perry Newman, CPC/CSMS. Executive Resume Writer/Career Coach.
> 25 years' experience.

LEADERSHIP SKILLS

Leadership is the most complex of all the *transferable skills* and combines all the others. As you develop *teamwork skills*, notice how you are willing to follow true leaders, but don't fall in line with people who don't respect you and who don't have your best interests at heart. When others believe in your competence, and believe you have everyone's success as your goal, they will follow you. When your actions inspire others to think more, learn more, do more, and become more, you are becoming a leader. This will ultimately be recognized and rewarded with promotion into and up the ranks of management.

- Your job as a leader is to help your team succeed, and your *teamwork skills* give you the smarts to pull a team together as a cohesive unit.
- Your *technical* expertise, *critical thinking*, and *creativity skills* help you correctly define the challenges your team faces and give you the wisdom to guide them toward solutions.
- Your *communication skills* enable your team to *buy into* your directives and goals. There's nothing more demoralizing than a leader who can't clearly articulate why you're doing what you're doing.
- Your *creativity* (discussed next) comes from the wide frame of reference you have for your work and the profession and industry in which you work, enabling you to come up with solutions that others might not have seen.
- Your *multitasking skills*, based on sound *time management* and *organizational* abilities, enable you to create a practical blueprint for success and your team to take ownership of the task and deliver the expected results on time.

Leadership is a combination and outgrowth of all the *transferable skills* plus the clear presence of all the *professional values* we are about to discuss. Leaders aren't born, they are self-made. And just like anything else, it takes hard work.

CREATIVITY

Your creativity comes from the frame of reference you have for your work, profession, and industry. This wide frame of reference enables you to see the *patterns* that lie behind challenges, and so connect the dots and come up with solutions that others might not have seen because they are too closely focused on the specifics of the issue and don't have that holistic frame of reference that enables them to step back and view the issue in its larger context.

There's a big difference between *creativity* and just having ideas. Ideas are like headaches: We all get them once in a while, and like headaches they disappear as mysteriously as they arrived. *Creativity*, on the other hand, is the ability to develop those ideas with the strategic and tactical know-how that brings them to life. Someone is seen as creative when his ideas produce tangible results. *Creativity* also demands that you harness other transferable skills to bring those ideas to life. *Creativity* springs from:

- Your *critical thinking skills*, applied within an area of *technical expertise* (an area where your *technical skills* give you a frame of reference for what works and what doesn't).
- Your *multitasking skills*, which in combination with your *critical thinking* and *technical skills* allow you to break your challenge down into specific steps and determine which approach is best.
- Your *communication skills*, which allow you to explain your approach and its building blocks persuasively to your target audience.
- Your *teamwork* and *leadership skills*, which enable you to enlist others and bring the idea to fruition.

Creative approaches to challenges can take time or can come fully formed in a flash, but the longer you work on developing the supporting skills that bring *creativity* to life the more often they *will* come fully formed and in a flash. Here are five rules for building creativity skills in your professional life:

1. **Whatever you do in life, engage in it fully.** Commit to developing competence in everything you do, because the wider your frame of reference for the world around you, the more you will see the patterns and connectivity in your professional world, delivering the higher-octane fuel you need to propel your ideas to acceptance and reality.

2. **Learn something new every day.** Treat the pursuit of knowledge as a way of life. Absorb as much as you can about everything. Information exercises your brain, filling your mind with information and contributing to that ever-widening frame of reference that allows you to see those patterns behind a specific challenge. The result is that you will make connections others won't and develop solutions that are seen as magically creative.

3. **Catch ideas as they occur.** Note them in your PDA or on a scrap of paper. Anything will do so long as you capture the idea.
4. **Welcome restrictions in your world.** They make you think, they test the limits of your skills and the depth of your frame of reference; they truly encourage *creativity*. Ask any successful business leader, entrepreneur, writer, artist, or musician.
5. **Don't spend your life glued to Facebook or TV.** You need to live life, not watch it go by out of the corner of your eye. If you do watch television, try to learn something or motivate yourself with science, history, or biography programming. If you surf the Internet, do it with purpose.

Building *creativity skills* enables you to bring your ideas to life; and the development of each of these seven interconnected *transferable skills* will help you bring your dreams to life.

> **Transferable skills.** The hiring managers I have worked with are diligent in screening for these skill sets.
>
> Denise Wilkerson, RN, CPC. Executive Search Director, Global Edge Recruiting. Medical devices, biotech, pharma, sales/marketing management. 14+ years' experience.

▶ **Professional Values**

Professional values are an interconnected set of core beliefs that enable professionals to determine the right judgment call for any given situation. Highly prized by employers, this value system also complements and is integral to the *transferable skills*.

MOTIVATION AND ENERGY

Motivation and *energy* express themselves in your engagement with and enthusiasm for your work and profession. They involve an eagerness to learn and grow professionally, and a willingness to take the rough with the smooth in pursuit of meaningful goals. *Motivation* is invariably expressed by the *energy* you demonstrate in your work. You always give that extra effort to get the job done and get it done right.

Commitment and Reliability

This means dedication to your profession, and the empowerment that comes from knowing how your part contributes to the whole. Your *commitment* expresses itself in your *reliability*. The *committed* professional is willing to do whatever it takes to get the job done, whenever and for however long it takes to get it done, even if that includes duties that might not appear in a job description and that might be perceived by less enlightened colleagues as beneath them.

Determination

The *determination* you display with the travails of your work speaks of a resilient professional who does not back off when a problem or situation gets tough. It's a *professional value* that marks you as someone who chooses to be part of the solution.

The *determined* professional has decided to make a difference with her presence every day, because it is the *right* thing to do, and because it makes the time go faster.

She is willing to do whatever it takes to get a job done, and she will demonstrate that determination on behalf of colleagues who share the same values.

Pride and Integrity

If a job's worth doing, it's worth doing right. That's what *pride* in your work really means: attention to detail and a *commitment* to doing your very best. *Integrity* applies to all your dealings, whether with coworkers, management, customers, or vendors. Honesty really *is* the best policy.

> **Ethics.** Successful professionals tend to want to do "what's right," while remaining open to hearing counter-opinions and considering consequences before decisions are made.
>
> Rick Kean, Consultant Emeritus, A. M. Hamilton, Inc. Staffing and training. 30+ years' experience.

Productivity

Always working toward *productivity* in your areas of responsibility, through efficiencies of time, resources, money, and effort.

Economy

Remember the word "frugal"? It doesn't mean poverty or shortages. It means making the most of what you've got, using everything with the greatest efficiency. Companies that know how to be frugal with their resources will prosper in good times and in bad, and if you know how to be frugal, you'll do the same.

Systems and Procedures

This is a natural outgrowth of all the other *transferable skills* and *professional values*. Your *commitment* to your profession in all these ways gives you an appreciation of the need for *systems and procedures* and their implementation only after careful thought. You understand and always follow the chain of command. You don't implement your own "improved" procedures or encourage others to do so. If ways of doing things don't make sense or are interfering with efficiency and profitability, you work through the system to get them changed.

Development of *transferable skills* and *professional values* supports your enlightened self-interest, because it will be repaid with better job security and improved professional horizons. The more you are engaged in your career, the more likely you are to join the inner circles that exist in every department and company, and that's where the plum assignments, raises, and promotions live.

Anyone seen to embody these *transferable skills* and *values* in their *professional persona* will be known and respected as a consummate professional.

That you have these admirable traits is one thing; that *I* know you have them, well, that's another matter. You need to:

- Develop these skills and values.
- Make them a living dimension of your professional persona.

- Understand how each enables you to do every aspect of your job just that little bit better.
- Reference them subtly in your resume and other written communications.
- Reference them appropriately in your meetings with employers as the underlying skills that enable you to do your work well.

Examples of your application of these skills or the impact of these values on your work can be used in your resume, cover letters, and as illustrative answers to questions in interviews. But most importantly, these skills must become a part of you, for they will bring you success in everything you do.

Resources

- You must follow up on the *multitasking* advice. You'll find these *transferable skills* and *professional values* referenced in all *Knock 'em Dead* books, but especially in the latest edition of *Knock 'em Dead: The Ultimate Job Search Guide*.
- You'll also find audio and further commentary at *www.knockem dead.com* on the career success pages and links to help you further develop the transferable skills.

CHAPTER 3

YOUR RESUME HAS TO BE A KILLER
FOR YOU TO SURVIVE

Your resume is the most important financial document you will ever own. It demands your undivided attention, because when it works, the doors of opportunity open for you, but when it doesn't work, you don't either.

Everything has changed in job searching over the past few years, so don't think you can squeak by with updating your existing resume, because I can guarantee you that it will be ineffective. Don't waste your time; invest in your future by developing a killer new resume for the new work world.

> **The biggest mistake is** thinking the resume isn't that big a deal and assuming you've written a masterpiece when in fact it's typically total garbage.
>
> Karen McGrath, PHR. Talent Acquisition Manager, Enterprise Rent-A-Car.
> 22 years' experience.

Just as technology has revolutionized your professional world, it has also rewritten the rules of job searching, because all recruitment has moved to the Internet. The ease with which we gather and distribute information means that many more resumes are received in response to a single job posting than ever before. Resumes no longer go to someone's desk for review; they disappear into resume databases, which can contain more than 35 million resumes.

> **Who gets hired and why.** The candidates that most closely match the job description on paper get the interviews, period. If your resume and cover don't hit 75% or better of the requirements of the position, you won't get an interview.
>
> Michelle Hagans, Recruiter, Anu Resources Unlimited. IT and medical. 20+ years' experience.

For anyone to actually review your resume, it will first have to be retrieved from the depths of the database by a recruiter using exactly the same tactics as you would use to execute a Google search.

Your resume and all your job search tactics need to adapt to the new realities: If your existing resume is written along standard lines, once it is loaded into a resume database, it will be lost forever.

What's Important in a Resume

Titles Are Important

Every product has a name ("Coke") or a title ("*Avatar*"), because that's what draws the reader/viewer/buyer in. When a headhunter, HR recruiter, or hiring manager logs on to a resume database to search for a resume, the first thing she does is type a job title into a dialog box.

Every product in the world struggling for attention amidst the 3,000-plus advertising images that bombard us every day has a name/title as its first line differentiator—every product in the whole wide world, that is, except *the most financially important document you will ever own.*

> **Layout.** I consider a resume visually first. I look for education, position titles, and companies. If I see things that I need, then I will read the resume.
>
> Jim Rohan, Senior Partner, J P Canon Associates. Supply Chain Management. 25 years' experience.

For some reason eight out of every ten resumes lack a target job title to give the reader (or that electronic database spider) a focus. They start with the contact information and then—without a target job title or any way to tell the reader what the document is about— plunge straight into an "Objective" section laying out what the writer *wants* in an employer and then continues with what the writer *thinks* is important. Eighty percent of resume writers, in other words, figure that everyone will *enjoy* plowing through their resumes, blindly hoping to luck upon what exactly it was they were being sold.

Keywords Are Important

> **Keywords** specific to your industry are absolutely critical if you want your resume to show up on database searches.
>
> Marjean Bean, CPC. President, Medit Staff. Information technology. 30+ years' experience.

Along with a job title, recruiters will search resume databases and social networking sites using keywords or search terms relevant to the position they are trying to fill.

A job posting very often reflects the exact wording of the internal company job description that was developed to define the job. This is how the employer prioritizes the job's needs, and these are the words used to express them. You can leverage this knowledge in your dealings with headhunters, corporate recruiters, and hiring mangers throughout the selection cycle, and, even before that, in your resume.

Because these words and phrases have real meaning to recruiters and hiring managers, they are the terms used when searching resume and social network databases. After a job title is typed into a dialog box, another box pops up and the recruiter types in the words and phrases that best capture the essence of that job: keywords from the Job Description.

Once programmed to search for a specific set of words, the software scours the database and builds a list of all the resumes (or profiles in the case of social networking sites) that contain *any* of the chosen *descriptors* or *keywords*. It then weights the list. Those resumes with *the most frequent use and greatest number of keywords* rise to the top of the list. Preference in the weighting system is given to words that come near the top of the page. Because *recruiters very rarely go beyond the top twenty resumes in a database search*, not enough relevant keywords or keywords in the right place means no human will review it.

If and when your resume reaches human eyes, the process is equally alarming. Recruiters will read resumes pulled from the database once, perhaps twice. The first reading is a skim that takes five seconds to a minute. The layout, font and font size, and overall visual accessibility of your resume are major factors in your presentation of yourself to recruiters. So no job title, focus, and/or lack of relevant, readily visible keywords likely means no second read. Your resume needs a relevant target job title that is focused on the target job's deliverables and contains keywords relevant to the execution of that job's responsibilities.

Given these considerations, the next read is more careful. Recruiters look to see if the resume's claims hang together and tell the story of someone who really *gets* the job. Recruiters and HR typically start with up to twenty resumes and prune it to a *long list* of usually 6–8 candidates who will be interviewed in some depth, and who, if they don't self-destruct, will have their resumes passed on to a hiring manager.

Managers hate reading resumes; they just want to hire someone and get back to work. Bear this in mind, because you will use the insight to great advantage in your resume and in preparing for job interviews. The manager then determines the *short list* of candidates he will interview face-to-face.

The point here is that there's no sense in creating a generic resume that tries to be all things to all people. A resume that tries to cram in everything you have done without any real focus is doomed to fail any of these initial hurdles, and failure at any one of these points means no interview and no job offer.

Even when your resume finally gets in front of human eyes, it has precious little time to make a convincing argument and win the more serious second reading that will lead to a telephone conversation. *The success of your entire job search depends on getting into conversation with people in a position to hire you, as quickly and as often as possible.* Your resume plays a major role in this process and it has to be up to the task. I have a solution that will guarantee this happens.

The Solution: Target Job Deconstruction

Target Job Deconstruction (TJD) will help you create a maximally productive resume, one that:

- Establishes an achievable goal for your search
- Provides a template for the story your resume *must* tell to be successful
- Therefore delivers a resume that will open the door for interviews
- Tells you exactly where the interviewers and their questions' will focus
- Prepares you for the questions they will ask, and how you will answer
- Gives you examples with which to illustrate your answers
- Draws a behavioral profile of the successful professional that everyone wants to hire
- Draws a behavioral profile of the failure that nobody wants to hire

In short, it helps define the *professional you*, MeInc's latest product offering.

> **Make it relevant.** I often find candidates who are very proud of their international experience, global! That's great, but if they took 10 seconds to think about OUR company they would know it isn't global. How easy a win this is if done right.
>
> Nancy C. Anton, CPC. Talent Consultant, CIGNA. 20 years' experience.

The TJD Sequence

Your resume will obviously be most effective when it starts with a clear focus and understanding of a specific target job. *TJD* allows you to analyze exactly how employers prioritize their needs for your target job and the words they use to express those needs, resulting in a detailed template for the story your resume needs to tell. When you have this focus, you can write the resume by first looking backward into your work history for those skills and experiences that best demonstrate your qualifications for the target job, then by expressing that experience and those skills in the words most likely to resonate with the recruitment and selection team.

Step 1: Decide on a Primary Target Job

Focus on a specific and realistic target job, one in which you can succeed based on the skills you possess today. Practically speaking, this means you need about 75 percent of the skills and experience to get your foot in the door. So of all the jobs you can do—and we can all do more than one—decide on the one that will be the easiest sell for you and the easiest buy for the employer.

If you have more than five years of experience, there are probably a couple of jobs you can do. More than fifteen years' experience, and there could be half a dozen jobs in which you can succeed. Rank these jobs based on their availability, remuneration, fulfillment, and potential for growth or shrinkage, as these factors match your unique requirements. This evaluation is to help you determine a *primary target job*.

This does not mean you cannot pursue any of those other jobs for which you have the desire and qualifications. It allows you to create your primary resume with a single *primary target job* in mind, the job that offers you the greatest chances of success!

CREDENTIALS, NOT POTENTIAL, WIN YOU JOB OFFERS

Some people think you change jobs to get a promotion, but this is largely incorrect, especially in a tight job market. *People get hired based on their credentials, not their potential.*

Most people don't get promotions to the next step on the professional ladder when they change jobs, because that would mean coming onboard as an unknown quantity in a job they've never done. Typically, most professionals accept a position similar to the one they have now, but which offers opportunity for growth once they have proved themselves.

CREATING JOB-TARGETED RESUMES FOR THOSE OTHER JOBS YOU CAN DO

Once you have a *primary* resume tailored to the most logical focus for your next job, you can quite easily customize it for any of those other jobs in which you are interested. Invariably there is overlap in the skills and experience demanded by the different jobs for which you are qualified. Consequently, you can take that primary resume, make a copy, retitle it, and, having completed the *TJD* sequence on that next target job, make the necessary changes to give your secondary resume the specific focus it needs. You won't have to start from scratch, and you'll have a customized resume for each opportunity you want to pursue.

Step 2: Understanding Your Target Job

Collect a half-dozen job postings for your primary target job. To help you do this quickly, use one of the job spiders listed in the Internet Resources at *www.knockemdead.com*. Each of them will search thousands of job sites for you. Some are free, and some are for a fee, but they all work similarly—the home page has a couple of dialog boxes: one for a job title and one for a geographic area. If you cannot find half a dozen jobs in your target location, just try another major metro area. For the purpose of *TJD* it doesn't matter where the jobs are located: You are just trying to get inside employers' heads and understand how they prioritize their needs for this job and the words they use to express those needs.

Put the job postings you find in a folder on your desktop. From these six job postings (the larger your sample the better) you will discover how employers think about, prioritize, and express their needs when writing job descriptions and hiring. The result will be a template that describes your target job *in the way employers themselves think about and describe it.*

Step 3: Look at Your Target Job from the Other Side of the Desk

This is where you deconstruct your collection of job postings to understand exactly how employers think about, prioritize, and describe the deliverables of your job.

1. Start a new Word document, and name it "Primary TJD" or something similar.
2. Under a first subhead entitled "Target Job Titles," cut and paste the variations on the job title you are pursuing from your collection of job postings.
3. Add a second subhead entitled: "Experience/Responsibilities/ Skills/Deliverables/Etc."

    Review your collection of job postings and find one requirement that is common to all six; of these six choose the most complete description of that particular Experience/Responsibility/ Skill/Deliverable and paste it under the second subhead and put the number 6 in front of it to signify that it is common to all six job postings. Underneath it list any different keywords used in the other five job postings to describe this same requirement.

    Repeat these steps for any other requirements that are common to all six of your collected job postings, placing the number 6 alongside each one.
4. Repeat this process for all requirements that are common to five of the six job postings, then four of the six postings, and so on down the line.

At the end of this first part of the TJD sequence you will be able to read the document and say, "When employers are looking for _____, these are the job titles they use; this is the order in which they prioritize the importance of their needs, these are the skills, qualifications, experiences, deliverables, and educational requirements they look for, and these are the words they use to describe them." As you read through your *TJD* document, the story your resume needs to tell will be laid out before you, and some of those promises I made a few paragraphs back will begin to sound a little less like smoke and mirrors.

Step 4: Identify What's Missing

Add to your *TJD* any additional skills/experiences you believe are relevant to this job. There are plenty of job descriptions that don't tell the whole story. In some companies, even publicly traded multinationals, the job descriptions can be maddeningly vague because the company hasn't paid close enough attention to the hard skills of the job. If you know a specific skill is mandatory for this job, feel free to add it at the bottom of your list. Job postings can also be vague or poorly thought through, which is why you collect a number of them and add responsibilities that you know belong.

Step 5: Problem-Solving

At their most elemental level, all jobs are the same—they focus on *problem identification, avoidance, and solution.* That you are able to *identify and solve* the problems that crop up in your area of expertise is a big part of turning job interviews into job offers, so building this awareness into your resume makes a lot of sense.

Go back to your *TJD* and start with the job's first requirement. Note the problems you will typically need to *identify, solve, and/ or prevent* in the course of a normal workday as you deliver on this requirement of the job. List specific examples, big and small, of your successful *identification, prevention, and/or solution to the problems.* Quantify your results when possible.

Repeat this with each of the *TJD*'s other requirements by identifying the problems inherent in that particular responsibility. Some of these examples may appear in your resume as significant professional achievements, while others will provide you with the ammunition to answer all those interview questions that begin, "Tell me about a time when. . . ."

Step 6: Achievements

Make a list of your greatest solo professional achievements from each of the jobs you have held, quantifying the results where you can, to demonstrate the value of your work. Add to this list examples of team achievements to which you contributed.

Once you have made this list, come up with a couple of examples of projects that went wrong and couldn't be fixed; you need these to illustrate your answers to questions that might well be asked about projects that went wrong. Ideally, you want examples that are in the past, where the failure was less than catastrophic, and where other people were involved, so you weren't solely responsible; in every example you must illustrate what you learned from the experience.

As interviewers are fond of asking you questions like the following, now is a good time to see if you can find examples to use in answer to these questions:

- Things didn't work out well (but did in end)
- Things didn't work out well ever; what you learned
- Unpopular decisions you have had to make
- How you developed new processes/ways (because existing ones didn't work or weren't efficient)
- How you improved something that was already working well
- How you fixed something broken

Give some thought to these examples as you do *TJD* and come back to them as you are preparing for an interview. This may seem like a lot of work, but the better prepared you are, the more job offers you will land and the better companies you will land those job offers with.

Step 7: A Behavioral Profile for Success

Interviewers always have an image of the person they want to hire (and the person they don't). This is not about height, weight, and hair color; it's a composite behavioral profile of the best people they've known in the job. It's what hiring managers want to find and will hire when they see it.

Have you ever thought about the behavioral profile that defines success in your area of expertise and then measured yourself against it? Doing so can help you define the professional you want to be and the persona you want to show to the professional world. Not understanding how your behavior can help or hinder your success usually means that you are unwittingly sabotaging future potential.

Work your way through each of the responsibilities itemized in your *TJD* one by one, profiling the *best* person you ever saw doing that aspect of the job and what made her stand out. Describe how she went about the work, skills hard and soft, interaction with others, general attitude and demeanor, and anything else that sticks out in your mind about that person, and you'll get something like: *Carole Jenkins, superior communication skills, always asking questions and listening, a fine analytical mind, great professional appearance, and a nice person to work with; she'd do anything for anyone.* Do this for each one of the job's deliverables and you will have a detailed behavioral profile of the person all employers want to hire and everyone wants as a colleague: *You will have a behavioral profile that will help you land job offers and, just as importantly, a behavioral profile for professional success.*

Step 8: A Behavioral Profile for Failure

Now think of the *worst* person you have ever seen for each of the requirements and what made that individual stand out in such a negative way. Describe the performance, professional behaviors, interaction with others, and general attitude and demeanor of that person and you'll get something like: *Jack Dornitz, insecure, critical, passive aggressive, no social graces.* You are describing the person that all employers want to avoid and no one wants to work with; and *you will have a behavioral profile for long periods of unemployment and professional suicide.* Then compare yourself against this profile and see if there is anything you need to change or work on.

Step 9: Transferable Skills and Professional Values

The final step of *TJD* is to review each of the skills/responsibilities/ deliverables of the job one last time to identify which of the *transferable skills* and *professional values* help you execute your responsibilities in each of the target job's responsibilities.

Once you complete and review your *TJD*, you will have a clear idea of the way employers think about, prioritize, and express their needs for this job; you'll know what they'll need to ask about at interviews and, beyond the hard skills, exactly the person they will hire. Yes, it will take time and it would be easy to cut corners or just skip it, but this is your career and this is your life: Make the choice that is right for your long-term success and happiness.

The more immediate result will be to give you a template for the story your resume has to tell, and an objective tool with which to evaluate your work. And when you apply what you learn from the *TJD* exercise to your professional life, it will increase your job security as it opens doors to the inner circles that exist in every department and company.

Building Your Resume

Once you have a clearly defined target job, you can look back into your work history and pull out the experiences that best reflect your ability to do this job. To help you gather and archive the right information you can download a resume questionnaire at *www.knockem dead.com*; there are also "find resume" templates available.

Five Rules for Building Great Resumes

1. Always use a Target Job Title. The Target Job Title appears at the top of your resume, immediately after your contact information, as a headline for the whole document.

2. Follow your Target Job Title with a Performance Profile *rather than a Job Objective or Career Summary.* This is because it speaks directly to the needs of the Target Job Title and because hiring managers link the phrase with performance reviews. Your *Performance Profile* should echo the most important deliverables of the job as determined by your *TJD* in the words identified as having most meaning to employers. The result is that your grasp of what's important in this work and your ability to do the job is immediately communicated along with the words that will have most resonance to the reader and most effect on the search engines.

> **Performance Profile.** If I can't see in about 10 seconds that you have at least 50% of the qualities I'm seeking for my client, I'm moving to the next resume. That's right, I said 10 seconds. A seasoned recruiter scans that quickly.
>
> Michelle Hagans, Recruiter, Anu Resources Unlimited. IT and medical. 20+ years' experience.

Capture the (approximately six) most important deliverables of the job, turning them into a short narrative, ideally no longer than five lines. If more than five lines, a second paragraph or bullets will enhance the visual accessibility that is so important to getting your message across.

3. A Core Competencies Section follows this. You identified a wide selection of the competencies required for this job in your *TJD*, and this part of your resume should list as many of them as you possess. You might also include any other skills that *you know to be relevant.*

> **Core Competencies and Resume Real Estate.** Search engines pay more attention to relevant keywords at the top of online profiles or web pages and rank web pages with better keyword density higher.
>
> Meg Guiseppi, C-level Executive Job Search Coach, Executive Career Brand. 20+ years' experience.

The following core competency section comes from a Hollywood Financial Analyst's resume:

Core Competencies		
✓ Research & Analysis	✓ Accounts Receivable	✓ Auditing
✓ Accounts Payable	✓ Journal Entries	✓ Royalties
✓ Payroll	✓ Financial Statements	✓ Licenses & Royalties
✓ General Ledger	✓ Artist Contracts	✓ Microsoft Office
✓ Escalation Clauses	✓ Equipment Leases	✓ Tracs
✓ Invoice Coding	✓ J.D. Edwards	
✓ Peachtree	✓ Bank Reconciliations	

This helps database visibility because it guarantees you are using the words employers use, and by getting them near the top of the page, you ensure they carry more weight with the algorithms of database search engines.

Following a Target Job Title and Performance Profile customized to that target job, your Core Competency section lists all the skills required to execute the responsibilities of the job. For the reader evaluating your resume, each word or phrase acts as headline for a topic to be addressed at the interview and increases the odds of that interview happening. It also means you have all the critical information an employer would need to screen you in the first half of the first page, which succinctly demonstrates your *critical thinking* and *written communication skills*.

You can repeat Core Competency keywords throughout the body of your resume within the context of each job in which you used them, doubling the number of relevant keywords and further improving your resume's performance with the resume database search engines.

4. Never put salary on a resume. If salary information is requested for a specific opening, put it in your cover letter or in a separate salary document attached to your resume. If you are earning too little or too much, you could rule yourself out before getting your foot in the door. Don't tie yourself to a specific figure: Give a range.

5. Keep your resume tightly focused. Tell what you can do but do not tell how you do it. This saves valuable space, and the *how* is more appropriate to the interview.

The age-old standard for resume length used to be one page for every ten years of experience, and never more than two pages. However, as jobs have gotten more complex, they require more explanation. For many IT people and professionals with significant experience of management in the higher ranks, a two-page resume is almost impossible to achieve. The length of your resume is less important than its relevance to the target job, and a two-page resume that has the right stuff, but is illegible because of layout and the ridiculously small font you had to use to squeeze everything onto two pages, doesn't advance your candidacy.

> **Length.** With most employers, the 1–2 page rule is irrelevant as resumes are initially screened via keywords and then accepted for phone screen. Following this outdated rule has caused more people to be overlooked than hired.
>
> Wendy Adams, Founder, The Career Coach. Transitions. 20 years' experience.

If the first page of your resume is tightly focused and contains a Target Job Title, a Performance Profile built on employers' on top priorities as determined by *TJD*, and a Core Competency section based on the same research and packed with relevant keywords, you will have the reader's attention by the time he gets halfway down the first page. When the first page makes a convincing argument, the rest of your resume will be read carefully. A longer resume also means that much more space for selling your skills with relevant keywords and that many more opportunities to establish your brand. (FYI, the higher up the ladder you climb, the more likely that 10-point fonts will cause eyestrain and won't be appreciated.)

Controlling Resume Length

While length doesn't matter as much as it used to, you should still make every effort to maintain focus and an "if in doubt, cut it out" editing approach. When keeping your resume pruned to a manageable length is an issue, remember that you can add the information you must cut to a more detailed social networking profile at LinkedIn.com or Facebook.com (social networking is addressed in Chapter 5).

> **It's important** to communicate within seconds. This is best done by using bullets to highlight your accomplishments.
>
> Denise Wilkerson, RN, CPC. Executive Search Director, Global Edge Recruiting. Medical devices, biotech, pharma, sales/marketing management. 14+ years' experience.

As you will see in some of the expert panelists' opinions, recruiters like to see these social networking links on your resume to find out more about you. So if there is "nice to have" but not "must have" information on your resume that is pushing you onto another page, cut it and add it to your LinkedIn.com profile.

Emphasize your achievements. Make your achievements visible with bullets and quantify them whenever you can. Always tell 'em what you've done, but never how you did it: That's for conversation.

> **The new one-page resume.** A multi-page document is a one-page document with attachments. That's why I add the following to the first page footer of every multi-page document: *"More indicators of return on investment **General Dynamics** can use. . . ."*
>
> Don Orlando, MBA, CPRW, JCTC. Owner, The McLean Group. Coaching senior executives. 17 years' experience.

Here is an example of a *Knock 'em Dead* resume: Job targeted, coordinated Performance Profile and Core Competency sections, with keywords repeated in context for high performance in database searches; clean businesslike layout and font choice, delivering instant visual accessibility for recruiters (resume templates and custom-built resumes like this available at *www.knockemdead.com*).

Patricia Johnson

Palmdale, CA 93550   Mobile (661) 555-9876   aaa_acountant@email.com

Financial Analyst

Performance Profile

Detail oriented problem-solver with excellent analytical skills and a track record of optimizing productivity, reducing costs, and increasing profit contributions. Well-developed team-building and leadership skills, with experience in training and coaching co-workers.

Works well with public, clients, vendors, and co-workers at all levels. B.S. in Finance, graduating with honors concurrent with full-time, progressive business experience.

Core Competencies

➢ Research & Analysis	➢ Accounts Receivable	➢ Auditing
➢ Accounts Payable	➢ Journal Entries	➢ RoyaltiesAuditing
➢ Payroll	➢ Financial Statements	➢ Licenses & RoyaltiesRoyalties
➢ General Ledger	➢ Artist Contracts	➢ Microsoft OfficeLicenses & Royalties
➢ Escalation Clauses	➢ Equipment Leases	➢ Microsoft Office
➢ Invoice Coding	➢ J. D. Edwards	
➢ Peachtree	➢ Bank Reconciliations	

PROFESSIONAL EXPERIENCE

MAJOR HOLLYWOOD STUDIO, Hollywood, CA   2000 to Present
Royalty Analyst—Music Group, Los Angeles, CA   2005–Present

Achieved fast-track promotion to positions of increasing challenge and responsibility. Process average of $8-9 million in payments monthly. Review artist contracts, licenses, and rate sheets to determine royalties due to producers and songwriters for leading record label. Ensure accuracy of statements sent to publishers in terms of units sold and rates applied. Research, resolve, and respond to all inquiries.

• Resolved longstanding problems substantially reducing publisher inquiries and complaints.
• Promoted to "Level 1" analyst within only one year and ahead of two staff members with longer tenure.
• Provided superior training to temporary employee that resulted in her being hired for permanent, Level 1 position after only three months.

Accounts Payable Analyst—Music & Video Distribution   2002–2005

Processed high volume of utility bills, office equipment leases, shipping invoices, and office supplies for 12 regional branches. Assisted branches with proper invoice coding and resolving payment disputes with vendors.

• Identified long-standing duplicate payment that resulted in vendor refund of $12,000.
• Created contract employment expenses spreadsheet; identified and resolved $24,000 in duplicate payments.
• Gained reputation for thoroughness and promptness in meeting all payment deadlines.
• Set up macro in accounts payable system that streamlined invoice payments.
• Consolidated vendor accounts, increasing productivity and reducing number of checks processed.

Accounts Receivable Analyst—Music & Video Distribution   2000–2002

Processed incoming payments; received and posted daily check deposits, reviewed applications for vendor accounts; distributed accounting reports and ordered office supplies. Handled re-billings of international accounts for shipments by various labels. Promoted to permanent employee from temporary after 90 days.

Additional Experience: Billing Clerk / Accounting Clerk / Bookkeeper (*details available upon request*)

EDUCATION

CALIFORNIA STATE UNIVERSITY, Northridge, CA   2005
B.S. in Finance; Graduated With Honors • *Completed Studies Concurrent with Full Time Employment*

Computer Skills: Windows, Microsoft Office (Word, Excel, PowerPoint), Peachtree, J. D. Edwards, Tracs

Cover Letters

The right cover letter can get your resume read with serious attention. Here is a cover letter known as an *Executive Briefing*. It works because it clearly matches your skills against the job's requirements and is visually accessible. Like many great ideas, the Executive Briefing is beautiful in its simplicity. The job's requirements are listed on the left side of the page, and your skills, matching those requirements point-by-point, are on the right,

From: A1coordpro
Subject: Assessment
Coordinator Date: February 28th, 2011 11:18:39 PM EST
To: jobs @******

Dear HR Staff,
Your posting for an Assessment Coordinator seems to perfectly match my background and experience. As the International Brand Coordinator for Kahlúa, I coordinated meetings, prepared presentations and materials, organized a major off-site conference, and supervised an assistant. I believe that I am an excellent candidate for this position, as I have illustrated below:

Your Requirements	My Qualifications
Highly motivated, diplomatic	Successfully managed project teams involving different flexible, quality-driven professional business units. The defined end results were achieved on every project.
Exceptional organizational skills and attention to detail	Planned the development and launch of the Kahlúa Heritage Edition bottle series. My former manager enjoyed leaving the "details" and follow-through to me.
College degree and 6 yrs exp.	BA from Vassar College, 6+ years relevant business experience in productive, professional environments.
Computer literacy	Extensive knowledge of Windows and Macintosh applications.

I'm interested in this position because it fits well with my new career focus in the human resources field. Currently, I am enrolled in NYU's adult career planning and development certificate program and working at Lee Hecht Harrison.

My resume, pasted below and attached in MSWord and as a PDF, will provide more information on my strengths and career achievements. If after reviewing my material you believe there is a match, please call me. Thank you for your consideration.

Sincere regards,

Jane Swift

> **Don't offer solutions to your perception of a company's problems.** People believe they look good by telling the company a better way to do their business. You cannot possibly know if your perception of a problem is correct. Your arrogance and lack of insight will upset more than it will impress.
>
> Paul Cameron, President, DriveStaff Inc. Technology recruitment. 14 years' experience.

An Executive Briefing is helpful in the screening process because it offers a concise picture of a thorough professional, in an easy-to-read format that details exactly how you match the requirements. It makes life easier for the reader by cutting directly to the chase. As you'll note in some of my colleagues' comments, making life easier for your boss is one of the considerations that help get you hired.

The Executive Briefing can help you at interviews too. Have you noticed that sometimes when you have meetings with a number of different people on the day of an interview *not all of your interviewers seem to know what job they are talking to you about*? Because an Executive Briefing so clearly matches requirements with your qualifications, it can quickly and diplomatically get everyone on the same page. Always take copies of your Executive Briefing to interviews along with your resume: This will ensure those additional interviewers have the right focus, and could be just the edge you need.

In addition to the cover letter, there are a number of other ways you can use written communication in e-mails and letters to increase your impact on people and improve your odds in the job search and interview cycle: broadcast and networking letters; follow-up letters after telephone interviews and face-to-face meetings; negotiation, rejection, and acceptance letters; as well as resignation and thank-you letters. They all have a role to play and you can find over a hundred templates for them at *www.knockemdead.com*.

> **How to name your resume docs.** Name it MARYSMITHresume. DOC—not MyBestVersion . . . Keepthisone . . . Resume4 . . . These things might mean something to you, but a recruiter will never find you again with that kind of document name.
>
> Nancy Schuman, CSP. Corporate VP Marketing, Lloyd Staffing. 30 years' experience.

Creating a brand-new resume for this job search will pay you back the moment you land that job, but using one of the job spiders mentioned earlier to monitor what new skills the market is demanding once or twice a year will keep your resume up to date and your professional development on track. This helps maintain a stronger grip on where your career is headed and how you are going to make the journey. There is much more that can be said about the crafting of effective resumes and job search letters. Here are further resources.

Resources

- You will find a complete discussion of all aspects of resume building in *Knock 'em Dead Resumes, 9th edition.*
- You will find a complete discussion of all aspects of job search letters in *Knock 'em Dead Cover Letters, 9th edition.*
- Never buy used job search and career books because they go out of date very quickly. *Knock 'em Dead* books are updated every year.
- You can find a downloadable MSWord resume questionnaire at *www.knockemdead.com* that will help you gather all the necessary information to build a killer resume.
- You can find resume templates and job search letter templates or invest in a professionally written resume at *www.knockemdead.com*.

CHAPTER 4

THE NETWORK-INTEGRATED PLAN
OF ATTACK

The biggest job search mistake. Not viewing job search as a job in itself. This is where taking responsibility for your life, becoming your own marketing expert comes into play.

Mike Squires, Senior Technical Recruiter, PayPal, an eBay Company.
15 years' experience.

Companies assess their staffing needs up to twelve months in advance, so the interviews you go on this year were mostly planned and budgeted toward the end of last year. Hiring budgets usually open at the start of the new calendar year with hires staggered throughout the year. The early part of every year usually has plenty of opportunity—so if you read this in November, you should be diligent about working on your job search right through the holiday season. Even with more jobs available there is a lot of competition, but with the right resume, job search tactics, and attitude, you will beat out your less savvy competitors.

The cost of hiring and training a new employee runs into thousands and often tens of thousands of dollars, so the entire recruitment process is cost/productivity conscious. Consequently, the people involved in a specific search—the hiring manager, corporate recruiter, and perhaps third-party recruiters (headhunters)—all want the same thing: good hires, fast hires, and hires made as cheaply as possible. Understanding how and why things are done, and in what order they are done, will help you focus your efforts on the most effective job hunting techniques.

A recruitment campaign generally goes as follows:

1. Look within the department, then the rest of the company. This could be a promotion for someone. Internal promotions are good for morale, involve no expenditure, cause less disruption, and are less risky than hiring someone from the outside, because current employees are a known quantity; knowing the culture, they will become productive more quickly. This is the easiest way to solve the problem.

   However, if ever anyone tells you that "we always hire/promote from within," they aren't thinking about the full implication of that statement: An internal promotion filling one open position usually means that a job opens up somewhere else within that company.

2. If there's no one within the company who can be promoted into the job, the next step is to ask, "Who do we know?" You'll put the word out to your staff and immediate peers.

3. If you are a smart manager you know that your reputation and your job ultimately rest on the productivity of the people you hire. You'll be actively involved in the search to whatever degree you can be, but you may well put the word out through your professional networks. Because your professional network will predominantly feature other professionals in your industry, they are likely to suggest qualified candidates, so you'll listen closely to what they have to say.

Tapping into the hidden job market? The more people in your network the greater the odds that they will bring unadvertised positions to your attention.

Perry Newman, CPC/CSMS. Executive Resume Writer/Career Coach. 25 years' experience.

4. HR will put together both an internal and an external job posting on the company website. Jobs often appear on company websites before they appear on commercial job sites.

These are the first steps of any recruitment campaign because they are fast, cheap, and because employees who come to the company "known by us" in some way are seen to be better hires and thought to get up to speed more quickly and stay with the company longer.

The next step—slightly more expensive and time-consuming—is to search outside the company for candidates who are unknown to the company. Candidates are sourced through advertising on commercial job sites (Monster.com/CareerBuilder.com), profession-specific job sites, and job boards on the sites of professional associations and societies. They are advertised on the social networking sites, which now almost all have job boards, and promoted through the special interest groups that feature so prominently on social networking sites.

Companies don't pay fees when people approach the company on their own, so they naturally look first and most favorably on applicants coming through referrals and the company website. This is also especially important in depressed economic times, when companies will often decide that they don't need to advertise with the big job banks because plenty of well-qualified and smart people will find their way to them. A preference for specialty and professional association job sites also makes sense: Fewer and better-qualified candidates can be expected to submit more consistently suitable resumes.

The people who have the most difficultly adapting are the baby boomers, or those who have been in the same company since the 1990s. To survive and compete, you must get a handle on job boards, specialty industry sites, social networking sites all play a part in the job search landscape.

Nancy Schuman, CSP. Corporate VP Marketing, Lloyd Staffing. 30 years' experience.

They *Want* to Hire You

Hiring managers hate recruitment and interviewing. All they want to do is find a productive *team player* as quickly as possible so that they can get back to the very pressing concerns of everyday business.

This means they are anxious to hire you as soon as they can find you. No one gets hired without conversations taking place, so your focus must be *to find and get into conversation with people in the recruitment and selection team as quickly and frequently as possible.* The major players in this world are, in order of priority:

1. The hiring manager
2. Professional colleagues of the hiring manager
3. Corporate recruiter
4. Professional colleagues of the corporate recruiter
5. Headhunters/Third-party recruiters

So, looking at how recruitment works, you have to ask yourself how to get into contact with these people as quickly as possible, which leads to four defining questions:

1. How do I get better connected to my local profession?
2. How do I get to know, and be known by, my peers?
3. How do I become more visible in my professional community?
4. How do I establish rapport with all these people and get them to help me?

This theme is central to the next three chapters, so I'll return to answering this question again and again, as will the rest of the gang.

> **Recruiters all over the world use social networking sites:**
> Facebook, Twitter and LinkedIn and using this as a tool to source candidates.
>
> Jackie Mills, Office Angels, Birmingham, United Kingdom. Administration recruitment. 14 years' experience.

Where Are the Jobs Today?

We live in a huge economy, so there are jobs at any time of year and in any economic climate. Even in the depths of the 2009/10 recession, there wasn't a month where we didn't see at least 4 million jobs posted on the Internet. The jobs are always there; you just have to find them.

Most of the attention in a typical job search is focused on the most established, major blue chip companies in the area, yet that isn't always where the best opportunities lie. About 90 percent of the growth in American business is in small companies with fewer than 500 employees. Not only that, the majority of the growth comes from small, young companies. The first 3–10 years of a company's existence are generally a period of particularly strong employment growth.

Small companies offer the opportunity to develop a wide range of skills quickly, to learn how companies work from a ringside seat. (Remember that dream of having your own business one day? Every day at work becomes on-the-job training for entrepreneurial enterprise.)

Smaller companies are more likely to recognize the worth of the deep and broad experience that comes with age; someone able to wear multiple hats is more often appreciated, as is your maturity and the mentoring skills you can bring to a job in this environment. Smaller, younger companies are also good for Generation Y, because that is where the growth and promotional opportunities are and where you can find great mentors from Generation X and the baby boomers.

Structuring Your Search

Today's employment market is different from anything that has existed in the past. It's faster, harsher, and more competitive. The speed at which information flies back and forth defies imagination. In this new world of work you can't rely on a single job search tactic, no matter how appealing it is to you. You'll need to weave together a number of strategies into a single cohesive approach, and this is what we begin to do in the next chapter.

CHAPTER 5

How to Build Networks for Today and Tomorrow

Employers prefer to hire people who come to them as a result of introductions, referrals, and recommendations, because they are seen to get up to speed faster, be more reliable, and stay with the company longer. This makes networking to get introductions, referrals, and recommendations a high-return job search strategy. It's also "warmer" than other tactics because the calls are friendlier and there's less chance of rejection—but you have been so busy working that you've never made much time to build and nurture networks. It's at times like these that you realize how important people are and vow to put more effort into building your networks and keeping in touch.

> **Networking** with people in your industry is the best way to find new employment.
>
> Al Daum, CPC. Alan N. Daum & Associates. Process automation engineering.
> 36 years' experience.

However, an approach of, "Hey Harry, How are you? We haven't spoken in ten years, you know where I can get a job?" is likely to fail. Networking is about sharing and giving, a *process* of building relationships over time, and your networks' effectiveness will reflect the effort you put into their development.

Types of Networks

There are two types of networks: professional and community.

A professional network is made up of professionals in your field from online social networking sites, professional, military, government, and college and high school alumni associations. Added to this are managers, coworkers from over the years, and other job hunters you run into along the way.

Community networks are built on family and relatives; friends and social interest groups; civic and spiritual associations; and service industry acquaintances like your banker, lawyer, plumber, etc.

If you're new to networking, at first it can seem like a big effort because it requires you to go outside your comfort zone and ask for help in all sorts of different situations. But in today's world, it's essential to develop this skill and much easier than in the past because everyone is more aware of the need for networking, and has either been in your situation, or knows that he will be.

Social Networking

Social networking via sites like Facebook.com and LinkedIn.com have transformed the way many people communicate. While Facebook.com is arguably the most visited website in the world, it is largely aimed at interactions between friends. LinkedIn.com, on the other hand, is the most important professional networking site for becoming visible to more headhunters and corporate recruiters.

If you're not a member, stop reading for a few minutes, go to *www.linkedin.com*, and sign up, then put my name in the search dialog box and invite me to be your first contact. Next, make a list of, and search for, past colleagues and managers you've worked with over the years; you'll probably find a few of them immediately. You'll be asked to create a profile as part of the registration process. Although they are known as "social networking" sites, you are involved in them for professional reasons, and this should inform everything you say about yourself. Try to use the content of your resume as much as possible, simply cutting and pasting it into your official profile.

Remember all that leftover information from the *TJD* that couldn't fit on your resume or didn't apply to that target job? It goes here. You make yourself visible, and because this is a social networking site and not a resume bank, you do so without an "I'm for sale" sign, which is useful when you are employed but looking for a new opportunity.

> **Your resume and LinkedIn profile** should say the same thing when it comes to dates, job titles, etc. Your resume should have a LinkedIn profile address—then your LinkedIn page offers more details and testimonials that speak to your skills, work ethic, and ability to get along with others.
>
> Nancy Schuman, CSP. Corporate VP Marketing, Lloyd Staffing. 30 years' experience.

If you don't use your resume word-for-word as your profile, take care that the same keywords appear. Just as you will search for others on the site using keywords, headhunters, internal recruiters, and hiring managers will be using keywords to search for you.

Digital Dirt

> **Digital Dirt.** Never complain about employers on Facebook or any other public forum. Increasing numbers of employees are getting fired for employer-bashing. Never even give the impression that anything is interfering with work.
>
> Janice Litvin, Executive Search Consultant, Micro Search. High-tech, marketing. 20 years' experience.

Headhunters and corporate recruiters are constantly on all social networking sites. They'll find you on LinkedIn.com and dig for more personal information on Facebook.com. If you have been involved with social networking since your up-all-night college days, go back now and clean up your digital dirt; some of those pictures from Spring Break might not represent the *professional you* in the most desirable light.

The best way to find a job today. Online identity management and search engine optimization can put you above the competition.

Olga Ocon, Executive Recruiter, Busch International. VP and CEO-level searches in high-tech. 15 years' experience.

Sites like LinkedIn.com are geared to professional networking. They feature job postings, special interest groups (including hundreds for job hunters), links to job boards, and local social events.

Perhaps the greatest asset of social networking sites is the way they allow you to find and reach out to exactly the kind of people with whom you need to be in communication. You can search the databases by name, job title, employer, company, location, or any keywords that might help you locate the right contacts. Almost all social networking sites now have job boards and lots of job hunter groups, and beyond these, there are even more professionally oriented special interest groups that help you connect with people who aren't looking for work but who want to discuss issues relevant to their profession.

There are too many social networks to list, and the more these sites proliferate, the more specialized they become. It is a good idea to have a presence on two of the biggest, LinkedIn.com and Facebook .com. Beyond this, go to *www.wikipedia.org* and search for "social networks" for a complete listing. You'll find networking sites by special interests, countries, sex, race, and more.

Professional Networks

Professional association membership is one of the best tools for job search and long-term career management. All professions and/or industries have at least one and sometimes many professional associations.

There are also associations that cater to all kinds of special interest groups. If you belong to one of these, there is likely an association that connects others like you in that same profession. If you can find a niche association that's a fit, join that as well: It represents another, even more finely tuned network that offers all the benefits we'll discuss.

When you connect with your professional community, you get to know all the most dedicated and best-connected professionals in your area, and in turn you become known by them. By belonging to one, you'll also reinforce your image as someone who's serious about *professional commitment*, an important element in the development of a professional brand, which we'll address shortly.

With professional associations, you can join a local or regional chapter or the national association; which you choose will depend on your pocketbook, and your need to reach more widely dispersed people in your profession.

Among the many other benefits of membership is the fact that employers post job openings to association websites. You can respond directly to the opening of course, but because you are an association member, you have access to the membership database and can probably find another member from that company who can give you an introduction (I'll show you other ways to leverage the membership database in the next chapter).

Attend the monthly meetings of the local chapter, circulate, and introduce yourself. You don't have to focus conversation on your need for a job—in fact, it's much better if you don't at first. Instead, talk about your work and get to know what other people do.

Associations function on volunteer power, so volunteer for one or more of its committees and offer to help any time the opportunity arises.

Associations all have newsletters and blogs, and the website usually has job postings along with other useful intelligence about your community. Membership will help you stay attuned to what is going on in your profession, and in addition you can take advantage of ongoing training and professional accreditations that make you a more knowledgeable and therefore a more desirable employee. Of course almost everything that is happening locally is also happening in the association's online groups.

For information about associations for your profession, the *Encyclopedia of Associations* is available online and at your local library. Or simply search Google for the name of your profession or industry followed by "association."

Alumni Associations

Just about every school has an association of past students. Up to now you may have ignored yours, since traditionally all alumni associations ever seem to do is ask for donations. While this is beginning to change as colleges recognize an ongoing obligation to their graduates, it is not the reason for my recommendation. You are not the only graduate to move on to a professional career, and your college alumni association can put you within reach of thousands of other graduates who will help you if they can, *just as you would help them, because of the shared college experience.* You'll be able to reach out to people with the same degree from the same school, working in companies all over the country and from the bottom to the top of the professional ladder.

Like professional associations, alumni groups will have a membership database, and there will almost certainly be a job search network and quite possibly job postings.

Corporate Alumni Associations

Larger corporations are also supporting alumni associations because it helps them stay in touch with once and future employees. Corporate alumni associations can be a useful way to gain contacts within one of your target companies.

Networking is about demonstrating to others that you are a contributor not taker.

Dr. Jim Bright, Partner, Bright & Associates, Australia. Author, *Chaos Theory of Careers*. 22 years' experience.

References

At the very start of your job search you should identify as many potential references as possible; the more options you have, the better the odds of coming up with excellent references. Re-energizing your relationship at the beginning of your search has other benefits:

- Reach out to all past managers (and coworkers), tell them you are involved in a job search, and ask if they would be willing to act as a reference when the time comes. Most people are flattered by the request and also pleased that you had the professional courtesy to ask them about it first. Since they can be encouraged to assist in your job search, learn what is happening in their lives, so that you can make a real effort to give as well as get.

- Tell them about the kind of job you are looking for. Beware of describing your *ideal job*, because that reduces their opportunities to help. Instead use your target job title and give a very brief description of the job as one in which you can use your _____ (here you describe your leading professional skills).

- Catching up with past managers and coworkers at their new companies can sometimes lead directly to interviews and job offers. As well as a potential reference, you have a contact who can tell you about their new employer's needs and culture, make introductions, and tell you how to make the best impression when interviewing there.

- After talking about their lives, ask if you can get their opinion on your resume. Most people like to be asked their opinion, but the real goal is to get your resume into the hands of people closely connected with the work you do. You'll show appreciation of course, but don't rush to revise your resume with every new opinion. Before implementing any advice remember that with the *TJD* process you created a resume carefully targeted to the needs of the job you are pursuing.

Establishing a web presence. People in their forties and beyond are often suspicious of social networking. LinkedIn provides you one instantaneously, so that when someone—a potential employer or a former colleague—Googles you, something will come up.

Allison Farber Cheston, Career Advisor, Allison Cheston & Associates. Author, *In the Driver's Seat: Work-Life Skills for Young Adults.* 28 years' experience.

When you are employed and looking for a new opportunity, don't use current managers and coworkers as references, because it could cost you a job. If you have only ever had the one job, people who have already left your current employer can be tracked down and will willingly become references; they might even make introductions for you with their current employer.

Intelligent Professional Networking

For networking to be productive, form relationships with people in your profession and industry at many levels. Almost anyone in your profession, industry, and location can be useful regardless of title or experience. However, the contacts who will be most helpful, *the high-value job titles*, will logically fall into these categories:

1. Those who are 1–3 title levels above you, as the people most likely to hire you now or in the future.
2. Those who are at your level with the same or similar job title, or 1–3 levels below you.
3. Job titles in other departments where their work involves interacting with your department.
4. Those who work in the same profession or industry but in other areas of expertise.

Networking depends on goodwill, so with all your networking contacts try to build a relationship by finding common ground. You can initiate relationships by asking for advice, and many people will give you a few minutes of their time. You will develop the best relationships by reaching out to others with help and advice, because when you offer good things, forging a relationship with you becomes important to the other person.

The challenge then becomes how to help, advise, or make a gesture that will encourage a relationship of introduction and job lead sharing. The answer is logical and painless: *Share the job leads you hear about that are inappropriate for your own use.* We'll pick up this idea in the next chapter when we talk about leveraging your job bank activities.

> **All things being equal,** job seekers with stronger web presence are noticed and chosen over those who have little or no presence online.
>
> Meg Guiseppi, C-level Executive Job Search Coach, Executive Career Brand. 20+ years' experience.

Personal Networks

Family and Friends

Who said, "Happiness is having a large, loving, caring, close-knit family in another city"? It was George Burns.

Your family is the most obvious component of your personal network, but also the easiest to misuse. Typically, family members understand next to nothing about what you do for a living and understand less than nothing about your professional world and career path. I was a working author for the last twenty years of my mother's life, and she always used to say, "I have no idea how you make a living when you only get one dollar from every book you write, so I always tell my friends you work in personnel . . . we understand that." It's easy to overestimate the knowledge family members have of your professional skills and just as easy to underestimate the value of their contacts. You need to use these insights to get the best from your social networks.

The members of your personal networks really want to help you, and although many of them still think of you as a snotty ten-year-old, given the right information they can be surprisingly helpful. Case in point, my crazy old mother had played bridge for years with another crazy old biddy in tweeds and twinsets. Said biddy knew someone who knew someone who knew the owners of a publishing company; my first foreign rights sale came from two ladies in their seventies who hadn't worked since the Second World War. So don't dismiss crazy old Aunt Aggie. She might be in a crochet group with all kinds of interesting people, and she's anxious to help if only you'll show her how.

Even if they have nothing to do with the professional world or like Mom and Aunt Aggie have only occasional contact with terrestrials, given the right guidance, your immediate family circle and your personal networks can cast a wide net and come up with useful leads. The problem is that it is easy to squander this potentially valuable resource by tapping into it too soon, before you have thought through how best to help your extended family help you.

Here are steps that make it easier for your loved ones to help you:

1. Think carefully about what you do for a living and put it in a one- or two-sentence description that even Aunt Aggie can grasp.
2. Think about the type of company you will work for and the kind of people you need to talk to. Condense this into simple terms and into a one- or two-sentence explanation: "I'm looking for a job with another computer company. It would be great if you or your friends knew anyone who also works with computers." Keep it real simple.
3. Give them the information you need to get in touch with these people: "All I need are the names, e-mail addresses, and phone numbers of anyone in these areas." (But maybe don't confuse Mom or Aunt Aggie with e-mail talk). "I'm not looking for someone to hire me; I'm just looking to talk to people who also work with computers."

This process of breaking your networking needs into *just three* simple statements gives your immediate circle something they can work with.

The same no-frills approach will work with little change with contacts in your other personal networks.

Civic, Social, and Spiritual Associations

Your local community is an important source of information, particularly, of course, for jobs that may be opening up in your area. The town council, Chamber of Commerce, Rotarians, Kiwanis, etc., are all potentially helpful, since they have a professional orientation. Church groups and school activities both offer a wide variety of people and activities. Don't buttonhole everyone at your first meeting with demands for information about job openings: Spend time getting to know them and becoming part of the group. Local networks take more time and effort, but they do result in jobs and they also involve you with the community at a difficult time in your life, when the inclination is sometimes to isolate yourself.

Social Interests and Hobbies

Get a life, get a hobby. Take up softball or tennis; start building model airplanes in your spare time. It doesn't matter what you do so long as it gets you out of the house and involves you with other people. Whatever interests you, finding other people interested in the same thing puts juice in your life, and some of these people will be or will know the people you need to know.

Your Job Search Network

You will sometimes feel that companies are looking for everyone but you; this can get depressing at times, so you need to be aware of the emotion and manage it. One way is to join or create a job search network with people in the same situation in your local community.

The Networking Mindset

Using your network to the best advantage means you've got to get in the right frame of mind. In every conversation you have, in every gathering of people you're at, your focus should be on how to grow your networks with the right kinds of people and how to gather useful information from the people you meet. If you come across someone who's working for a company you're interested in, ask some or all of the following questions:

- "What needs does your company have at present?"
- "Who in the company is most likely to need someone with my background?"
- "Who else in the company might need someone with my background?"
- "Is the company/department planning any expansion or new projects that might create an opening?"
- "When do you anticipate a change in the company's manpower needs?"
- "Does your company have any other divisions or subsidiaries? Where are they?"
- "Do you know any headhunters who work in this area?"
- "Have you heard of any companies in the area who are looking?"

Be sure to thank the other person for any information he gives you. In fact, send a follow-up e-mail thanking him. That properly expresses your appreciation and keeps your name front and center in his mind.

The quality of help you receive from your network contacts depends on the value you bring to each relationship. While you want answers to the above questions, that doesn't mean they are the first questions you ask.

How can I get them to talk to me? Offer value. Give them a reason to want to talk with you. Ask them what they need. Don't worry about what you need, you will get to that in time. Have something to tell them.

Nancy C. Anton, CPC. Talent Consultant, CIGNA. 20 years' experience.

In a job search you come across insights that are of interest to anyone in a job search and some of it just as interesting to anyone in your profession, whether they are job hunting or not. If you try to help everyone you talk to by showing an interest in their lives and needs, you will be the big winner. More on how to do this in the next chapter.

Resources

- Networking letters and resume templates can be found at *www.knockemdead.com*.
- Links for college alumni associations at *www.knockemdead.com*.
- You can learn more about networking in *Knock 'em Dead: The Ultimate Job Search Guide*, latest annual edition.
- For Internet resources to aid networking go to *www.knockemdead.com*, then to the Career Advice pages: Click on *Secrets & Strategies* where you will find the Internet Resources link.

CHAPTER 6

JOB SITES, RESUME BANKS, HEADHUNTERS, AND DIRECT RESEARCH

In a competitive job market, you cannot rely exclusively on networking or any other single job search tool. Along with networking, leveraging job sites, resume banks, and headhunters, direct research and approach are the most effective ways of finding opportunities. All these approaches work, but you cannot predict which approach will work for you, so you have to use them all.

Job Sites and Resume Banks

There are so many thousands of job sites, you could never hope to visit them all, and so you have to integrate the job site/resume bank aspect of your search intelligently. Start by identifying which sites are relevant to your search: In the Internet Resources appendix at *www .knockemdead.com* you can find job sites for many different professions. You should also utilize the job site aggregators/spiders mentioned in Chapter 3.

Your intent is to create a gradually growing database of job sites that generate job postings relevant to your needs. Take a day to visit job sites, starting with the listings I've just mentioned: Does the site have job postings that are suitable for you? If not, you can move on to the next site. If it does, you will want to register with the site to receive e-mail job alerts when new jobs matching your criteria get posted to the site.

As we discussed in Chapter 5, use your resume to create your profile. When you are asked about relocation and geographical preference in the registration process, leave these issues "open."

- It's better to reject an opportunity than never to hear about it.
- *Your weakest professional survival skill is also the most critical to your professional survival and success: turning job interviews into job offers.* Every opportunity to build skills and experience here should be seized, even if you don't want the job.
- We'd all move to Possum Trot, Kentucky, for the right opportunity and package.

> **Filling out an online application** using no capitals and no punctuation will get you nowhere.
>
> Michelle Hagans, Recruiter, Anu Resources Unlimited. IT and medical. 20+ years' experience.

When you are asked to define the jobs that interest you, keep your parameters wide. It is better to plow through a little junk than miss a great opportunity. You *could* then narrow your parameters to get better matches and weed out the nonsense over time. But before you do, remember that those jobs that aren't quite right for you could be just right for your networking contacts.

> **Job Search Failure?** If you're spending all or most of your time responding to job board postings and waiting to be offered interviews, chances are, not much is happening.
>
> Meg Guiseppi, C-level Executive Job Search Coach, Executive Career Brand. 20+ years' experience.

If a site has suitable jobs for you, other sites it is linked to might also be useful; check the partners/links pages. If these links aren't obvious, look for a site map, often in those links that always crowd the very bottom of the page.

Googling for Jobs

Google your target job title(s) and dig down for as many pages as it takes to run out of job sites. Most people get bored after the first couple of pages of a Google search, but you should be able to drill down ten or twenty pages and still find jobs, job sites, headhunters, and employers. Also try Googling with minimal keywords and restrictions. You may get a wider range of results, the vast majority being for jobs that hold no immediate interest. However, apart from a few relevant jobs, those results will reveal relevant job sites, employers, recruiters, and some jobs/job resources that could be helpful to networking contacts.

Resume Banks

The job sites will also have resume banks, so it's likely that the HR recruiters who are posting job openings to that site are also searching the resume bank.

Recruiters pay for access to resume banks, so the job sites tend to purge old resumes, usually every 90–120 days, so you'll have to go back periodically and repost your resume. Recruiters visit these sites regularly and are usually offered a tool to view resumes *by posting date*, enabling them to restrict their searches to only the most recent resumes. If you don't want to be overlooked, go back every week or two to update your resume. Keep a list of keywords (from job postings) that describe skills not currently listed in your Core Competency section: This gives you a meaningful way to update your profile. The site sees any change as a new resume being posted. You will want to add a few new job sites and resume banks to your job search database every week.

On the whole, corporate recruiters who advertise on a site will access its resume bank. Access to resume banks carries a fee. Headhunters, who spend most of every day roaming the Internet, and for whom the cost of subscribing to every resume bank would be prohibitive, prefer social networking sites. To become visible to headhunters you need to have a professional presence on LinkedIn.com and Facebook.com.

If the resume bank requires you to enter your document in ASCII format, go to *www.knockemdead.com* for a simple, step-by-step explanation of creating ASCII format resumes.

Headhunters and Other Recruiters

"Headhunter" is an apposite term. In days of old, humans proved individual superiority by physical strength; today it is done with brainpower. That's what headhunters do: They hunt heads, searching for the best brainpower available for their clients. In the process they execute the most sophisticated sales process on the planet: They sell products that talk back.

Here's a basic breakdown that will give you a realistic idea of what to expect from the different players in the recruitment field:

Headhunters work exclusively on behalf of employers, locating hard-to-find professionals for those clients. They do not find jobs for you; it is not what they are paid to do.

> **Recruiters love solid resumes.** Send a clean version of your resume with concrete information about your accomplishments. If you are a sales professional, sales numbers show your abilities.
>
> Denise Wilkerson, RN, CPC. Executive Search Director, Global Edge Recruiting. Medical devices, biotech, pharma, sales/marketing management. 14+ years' experience.

The headhunters who work on a retainer basis (the employer pays money up front) tend only to recruit at the higher executive levels. They specialize in professions and job categories within those professions on a regional, national, or global basis, and when recessions reduce the availability of retained searches they work on contingency searches.

Headhunters who work on a contingency basis (the employer pays money only when a position is filled) recruit at all levels for which an employer is willing to pay a fee—usually for professionals with three or more years' experience.

Private employment agencies typically fill lower-level positions with local companies and don't recruit, except when fees and opportunity make it worthwhile.

State employment agencies help people at all levels in the local community find jobs. In other words they do what the other guys do, but for free. However, because they are paid to help people find work rather than help the company find exactly what they want, state agencies don't enjoy the same relationships with employers that the headhunters do. On the plus side, most job openings get listed with state agencies, and because they have a national network, your local agency can link you to resources on the other side of the country. State employment agencies are the *only* ones focused entirely on helping you.

Your Approach

The higher up the professional ladder you are, the less likely local and state employment agencies will be able to help. Most professional people are best served by making contact with the headhunters. Whether a headhunter is contingency or retained doesn't matter to you: What matters is whether she specializes in searches within your professional area and your level. You just have to start making contact.

- There are a dozen headhunter databases comprising thousands of companies at *www.knockemdead.com*. You can find them on the job search advice pages. These will help you identify headhunters by location and professional specialization.
- Google your Target Job Title(s) and drive down through the pages. You'll find relevant jobs and will therefore visit the headhunter's website and upload your resume.
- You should also search the membership databases of your social networking and professional/alumni/corporate association websites, using terms like "recruiter," "headhunter," "recruitment," and "employment."

Headhunters won't find you a job, but if they have assignments you fit, be cooperative, keep your commitments, and never lie or prevaricate. You should always try to help headhunters, because it keeps you on their radar.

Direct Research—The Hidden Job Market

> **How do I get the attention of a corporate recruiter?** Target a desirable company. Research the players within the organization. Once you have compiled a list of the internal employees, search within their profiles for a shared or common acquaintance. If you have a shared acquaintance, I suggest reaching out to that employee prior to engaging with the recruiter. A referral from an internal employee gets noticed before anyone else does.
>
> Mike Squires, Senior Technical Recruiter, PayPal, an eBay Company. 15 years' experience.

Direct research enables you to tap into the hidden job market, finding all those jobs that you haven't been able to discover with your other job search strategies. Tapping into the hidden job market, as it's mysteriously referred to, is pretty straightforward.

More Jobs and More Employers Are Hiding in Plain Sight

You have already identified the most obvious potential customers by searching job banks and responding to appropriate job postings from employers in your target location. But are the only possible jobs and the only possible employers those you have already seen on the job banks you happen to frequent? Of course not.

It is logical that a company hiring other titles, and especially other titles in your department, or titles that interact with your department, might also be looking for someone like you. The following high-value job titles are always worth watching for when you visit job banks because job postings for other titles in your immediate area increase the odds of *your* job title being sought either now or in the immediate future.

- Job titles 1–3 levels above you
- Job titles 1–3 levels below you
- Other job titles in the same department
- Job titles in departments that regularly interact with yours

You can use postings for these high-value job titles in a few ways:

1. They identify companies that hire professionals like you.
2. They lead you to a company website. Read the other listed job postings; if there is a posting for you, respond to it. If not, upload your resume anyway.
3. The job postings for these high-value job titles are exactly the same high-value job titles you focus on in your networking activities: The people who would most appreciate knowing about these jobs are the same people most likely to know about jobs for you, and consequently most capable of giving you leads, introductions, and referrals. Pass on these leads, build goodwill, and they will likely return the favor.

> **An estimated 85 percent of $100K+ jobs** that are filled are not advertised and not posted on a job board—these are hidden jobs. Yet as many as 85–90 percent of executives are competing for that mere 15 percent of jobs that are advertised and visible.
>
> Meg Guiseppi, C-level Executive Job Search Coach, Executive Career Brand. 20+ years' experience.

Company Research Resources

Online and local library-based resources are a valuable supplement to the information you gather about potential employers from job banks and networking. There are many great job search tools that have been designed for other business uses; for example, Standard & Poor's (S & P).

S & P identifies every publicly traded company in the world and indexes them by industry, location, and in countless other ways. The information is detailed, telling you what the company does, providing contact information, and including a listing of key executives at the VP level and above. They even have a database of executives organized by name, personal information (schools, graduation dates, interests, clubs, etc.), title, and contact information.

If you use these research tools along with cross-referenced job postings, as described, you will have a complete picture of all the employers in your target location that could possibly need someone with your professional expertise.

This builds a database for your industry/specialty/profession that will help you tap into the hidden job market. And because the statistics say this might not be your last job search, gathering and saving all relevant information on employers you find now will give you a jump on the next one.

Resources

- You can find much more information on job search tactics in each of these areas, plus others, including job fairs in *Knock 'em Dead: The Ultimate Job Search Guide* (latest annual edition) and at *www .knockemdead.com* on the job search advice pages.
- Cover letter and other job search letter templates are also available at the website.
- You can find an extensive listing of direct research resources on the Internet Resources page at *www.knockemdead.com*. They can help you identify the full roster of potential employers in your target location, and they will all, to a greater or lesser degree, identify the names of senior management by title.

CHAPTER 7

REACH OUT AND TOUCH SOMEONE

Little happens in the professional world without conversations taking place; in job searches neither interviews get scheduled nor job offers made without them. That's why the focus of your job search is always to *get into conversation as quickly and as often as possible with the people who can hire you.*

Despite everything you've done up to now, nothing is going to happen without you getting into conversations with these people. You can wait for these conversations to happen or you can make them happen.

Best way to find a job? Talk to people.

Faith Sheaffer-Polen, Senior Career Coach, CareerCurve. Organizational psychology. 15 years' experience.

Sales and Marketing Strategies

You've posted your resume—on resume banks, and as your social networking profile on LinkedIn.com, etc.—and sent it in response to company and headhunter job postings. Every one of these resumes acts like a baited fish hook, but while positioning your resume where it can be seen is a sensible marketing tactic, just sitting back and waiting for a bite isn't the best way to land your next job.

> **Best way to find a job?** Get on the phone and out to networking events. The job market is only hidden from people who aren't out there *talking* about it.
>
> Paul Cameron, President, DriveStaff Inc. Technology recruitment. 14 years' experience.

Jobs in sales exist to generate revenue by getting into conversation with customers and selling them the product. Because marketing alone is never enough for profitability, MeInc too needs a sales operation to get into the conversations that lead to meetings, then negotiations, contracts, and the sale. Your successful job search, like any sales campaign, depends on *you getting into conversation, as quickly and as often as possible, with the people/job titles that can make the decision to hire you.*

Who to Approach Within Your Target Companies

Your identified target market should include every company within the geographic boundaries of your job search that could possibly hire someone like you. But companies aren't enough; you need to find people within those companies to talk to.

Getting into conversation with the people who have the authority to hire you is the central goal of all your job search strategies. It is the most effective way to get job offers and the activity that job hunters most want to ignore, because talking to strangers on the telephone suddenly seems like a scary thing to do. It's not scary; you do it all the time.

Before you get into conversation you have to identify whom you want to talk to and how to find them. The people you want to *reach as quickly, directly, and often as possible* are people holding those titles most likely to have the authority to offer you a job; typically these high-value target hiring titles are 1–3 levels above your own and in the same department or functional area. *The primary goal of your job search every day is to identify and get into a conversation with anyone who holds any of these target titles at every company in your target location.*

> **Getting through to power players.** People talk to me if I've sent them an e-mail that piques their interest on a subject that matters to them. You can usually get me to talk to you if you send me a well-written e-mail first, then leave a polite phone message late at night on my office phone. I read you, listen to you, and then I call back. But leave me a million messages and I won't call back.
>
> Nancy Schuman, CSP. Corporate VP Marketing, Lloyd Staffing. 30 years' experience.

- Corporate recruiters; because they are involved in the recruitment and selection cycle, they have a direct relationship with the hiring manager and a stake in completing searches in a timely and efficient manner.
- Titles 1–3 levels above your own in departments that have ongoing activities with your department. These people are the peers of the titles that will hire you and because of their continuing relations with your department are both likely to know of needs and able to make referrals.
- Titles similar to and 1–3 levels below your own, because these people either have jobs in the departments where you might like to work, or are looking for jobs in the same general area themselves.
- Titles of people in other departments or at other companies that had ongoing communication with you and your title.

Put these titles together and you have a hotlist of at least ten *high-value job titles* that represent the people who have the greatest odds of knowing about suitable jobs for you, being able to make the right introductions, and/or of hiring you. These are the people you want to *get into conversation with as quickly and as often as possible.*

The above titles represent the people you want to develop networking relationships with; they also represent the titles of job postings you'll stumble across and should snag.

Tools for Finding Names of Hiring Managers

Cross-reference your target companies with the members of your social networks to get referrals and introductions. Look for these employers and for your identified high-value networking titles in the special interest groups you belong to on social networking sites and use the common interest of the group to make an initial connection.

You can find a wide array of online search tools to find people by name, job title, company, industry, and location at *www.knock emdead.com*. Go to the Career Advice pages, then click on *Secrets & Strategies*, where you will find the Internet Resources link.

> **Six degrees of Kevin Bacon.** Most people are connected in some fashion, through social networking sites, churches, or your mother's friends' son.
>
> Mike Squires, Senior Technical Recruiter, PayPal, an eBay Company. 15 years' experience.

You can also use search engines to find job titles and names. Here's an example of how a professional in pharmaceutical sales looking to make direct contact with hiring authorities for a job at a specific company in the Pittsburgh area might approach keyword searches.

If you started with Google.com, you would do searches for each of the job titles 1–3 levels above your own. Each search would include one of these target hiring titles plus:

- Pharmaceutical sales (company name)
- Pharmaceutical sales (company name) Pennsylvania
- Pharmaceutical sales (company name) Pittsburgh
- Pharmaceutical Mgr sales (company name) Pennsylvania
- Pharmaceutical Mgr sales (company name) Pittsburgh
- Pharmaceutical Director sales (company name) Pennsylvania
- Pharmaceutical Director sales (company name) Pittsburgh
- Pharmaceutical VP sales (company name) Pennsylvania

Then:

- Repeat all without "pharmaceutical"
- Repeat all without company name
- Repeat with just the job title
- Then repeat with separate searches for the target hiring title plus: "hired," "resigned," and "deceased."

> **Ideas for tapping the hidden job market?** Get referred through your network. Many jobs are filled without being advertised. Make connections and hear about these openings from those who respect and want to work with you.
>
> Nancy C. Anton, CPC. Talent Consultant, CIGNA. 20 years' experience.

Once you've completed searches based on the target hiring titles, repeat the whole process as a Google News search. A "news" search looks for mentions of those keywords in media coverage; if you haven't used it before, the "News" tab is on the Google.com navigation bar between the "Maps" and "Shopping" links.

Doing news searches, you find names and titles plus information that you can use as a conversational icebreaker in your e-mail or conversation. Copy an interesting, relevant article and attach it in an e-mail. With a traditional letter, enclose a copy of the article. In both, your letter will open with mention of the media coverage, and this alone guarantees the rest of your message will be read. It is even more effective when you use it to open a telephone conversation: "I've been meaning to call you ever since I saw the article in. . . ."

> **Why do people talk to you?** I don't pass along useless or poorly thought out information so when people talk to me they walk away enriched.
>
> Perry Newman, CPC/CSMS. Executive Resume Writer/Career Coach. 25 years' experience.

When you know who you want to talk to and why and have the means of contributing to the relationship, your irrational fear of talking to strangers on the phone should begin to evaporate. Using these networking and direct research strategies to find the names that go with these *high-value job titles* will generate plenty of people to approach.

Capture Information

Capture the information you gather so that you can access and use it in this job search, and perhaps for other job searches down the road. If you stay in this profession and location, most of these companies are still going to be there and many of the people you find will too; and these companies and these people are still going to be hiring people like you. Capturing the information is another way in which you become knowledgeable about your profession and connected to the other players.

> **How do you get a foothold in the hidden job market?** Compile a list of 10–20 target companies that are a mutual good fit. Find one or two key people within each company. Connect with your key people through cold contact, an introduction, social networks, and/or other networking methods.
>
> Meg Guiseppi, C-level Executive Job Search Coach, Executive Career Brand. 20+ years' experience.

Beware Dream Employers

As you build these dossiers of information about individual companies in your target area, one or more of them will emerge as dream employers. Beware of applying for jobs at these "super desirable" employers right at the start of your search. Most likely your resume and interviewing skills are not up to speed at the beginning of your search. The last thing you need to do is fumble an opportunity to join the company of your dreams. It is better to hold off until you know that your resume is fine-tuned and that you won't swallow your tongue in the first few minutes of the interview. Then, when you feel confident, use network contacts to get insider information and referrals, and your approach to that dream employer is likely to be a smoother experience.

How to Quadruple Your Chances of an Interview

The more ways you approach your target companies and hiring managers, the faster you will *get into conversation with the people who can and will hire you*. Let's say you respond to a job posting by uploading your resume; that gives you one chance of getting an interview.

You can quadruple your chances of an interview if you also:

- E-mail your resume directly to the manager by name with a personalized cover letter. This alone will double your chances of an interview.
- Send a resume and personalized cover letter to that manager by traditional mail, and you will triple your chances of an interview. Don't smirk at the idea of traditional mail. We all like a break from the computer screen, so delivering your sales message and resume this way can be very effective. When you do this, note in the cover letter that you sent the resume by e-mail and that this additional approach is because you are really interested in the company and "wanted to increase my chances of getting your attention." Doing this demonstrates that you are creative and not a technological Neanderthal.
- Make a follow-up telephone call to that manager first thing in the morning, at lunchtime, or at 5:00 P.M. (when he is most likely to be available and picking up his own phone) and you will quadruple your chances of an interview.

Remember, a successful job search is all about *getting into conversation with people in a position to hire you as often as possible*. The more frequently you get into conversation with managers whose job titles signify that they have the authority to hire you, the faster you will land that new position, because you have skipped right over the hurdle of being pulled from the commercial resume database; you have sidestepped the corporate recruiter's evaluation process, and *as a result* you have the attention of the actual decision-maker and the chance to have a conversation, to make a direct and personal pitch.

Getting a resume to someone by name with a personalized pitch gives you a distinct advantage, never more important than when the economy is down or in recovery. At such times your competition is fierce and employers actually do recognize and appreciate the initiative and motivation you display by doing these things, especially picking up the phone and calling: All these approaches act as differentiating factors in your candidacy.

Initiating Conversations with Hiring Managers

Phone conversations are more powerful than resumes, e-mails, and letters, and they are essential to getting you interviews. Talking with high-value titles who haven't seen your resume, and following up on resumes you send out with a phone call, is the best way to get the interviews that lead to job offers.

Job search and career management is a huge and complex topic, and just reaching out and making contact is almost an entire book in itself. It includes:

- Finding e-mail addresses and telephone numbers for the names and titles you've identified
- Getting past gatekeepers
- Planning what you are going to say, recognizing the buy signals, and handling any objections that come up in the ensuing conversation
- Getting leads on other jobs and introductions to other managers if this contact doesn't pan out

These are all things you have to learn to do in executing a successful job search and learning to manage your career. I don't have the space to cover all these topics in this book, but anything I can't cover here, I'll provide resources for at the end of the chapter.

At the same time you are uploading to resume databases and e-mailing and traditionally mailing your resume to high-value contacts and hiring managers you identified today, pick up the phone and introduce yourself to the ones you identified and approached with a resume a day or two ago. Make as many of these calls as you send e-mails and traditional letters pitching your resume. The more often these conversations happen, the more quickly your search will end in success, and this extra step is never more important than during an economic downturn.

Don't deceive yourself by thinking this part of the search is not possible because you are terrified of picking up the phone to call strangers. We all talk on the phone all the time—these are just calls with a distinct purpose. It is something you can learn to do successfully, and whatever small pain it causes is far outweighed by what you gain: a new job and a fresh start on managing your career more successfully.

If you have just a single goal when you pick up the phone—get an interview—you have just one chance of success but many more for failure. But if you have multiple goals for your call, you have multiple chances for success. When headhunters make sales/marketing calls, they usually have five goals in mind. I have adapted the headhunter's goals to fit your needs in a job search:

1. I will arrange an interview date and time.
2. If my contact is busy, I will arrange another time to talk.
3. I will develop leads on promising job openings elsewhere in this and other companies.
4. I will leave the door open to talk with this person again in the future.
5. I will send a resume for subsequent follow-up.

Keep these goals in mind every time you talk with someone during your job search, because every conversation holds the potential for turning into an interview or leading you toward another conversation that will generate first a phone conversation then a face-to-face meeting.

You might worry about calling people directly because you are concerned that they will be annoyed by the perceived intrusion. This is a misconception: The first job of any manager is to get work done through others, so every smart manager is always on the lookout for talent, if not for today, then for tomorrow. If that isn't enough to allay your fears, keep in mind that the person on the other end of the line has very possibly been in your position and is sensitive to your situation. If you can be concise and professional, you'll find that the great majority of people you contact will try to be helpful.

Paint a Word-Picture

The secret is being succinct. With an initial introduction and presentation that comes in at well under a minute, you won't be construed as wasting anybody's time. Your aim is to paint a representation of your skills with the widest appeal while keeping it brief out of courtesy, as well as to avoid giving information that might rule you out.

Step 1

Give the employer a snapshot of who you are and what you do. The intent is to give that person a reason to stay on the phone. You may sometimes have an introduction from a colleague, in which case you will build a bridge with that:

"Miss Shepburn? Good morning, my name is Martin Yate, and our mutual friend Greg Spencer suggested I call. . . ."

Or you may have gotten the name and contact information from, for example, a professional association database, in which case you will use that as a bridge:

"Miss Shepburn? My name is Martin Yate. We haven't spoken before, but as we are both members of the _____ association, I hoped I might get a couple of minutes of your time for some advice. . . ."

Never ask if you have caught someone at a bad time because that's offering your contact an excuse to say she is busy. On the other hand, asking whether you have caught someone at a good time will usually get you a positive response, or just pausing after stating the reason of your call will work. Then you can go into the rest of your presentation. If at any point your contact says or implies that he is harried, immediately ask when would be a good time to call back.

Now we come to the meat of your presentation. Grab the listener's attention now and you are off to a good start. You want to capture a complete picture of the *professional you* in less than one minute, ideally less than forty-five seconds, and the good news is that you already have the text for what you need to say.

In creating your resume you completed *TJD* exercises that helped you prioritize employers' needs for your job title. When you got to writing the Performance Profile for your resume, which introduced the *professional you* succinctly, you condensed the leading employer priorities into three to six short sentences. So you already know which aspects of your experience have the widest and most relevant appeal, and we just have to retool them for speaking rather than reading; that's easy. After your introduction:

"Miss Shepburn? My name is Martin Yate. We haven't spoken before, but as we are both members of the _____ association, I hoped I might get a couple of minutes of your time for some advice. . . ."

You pause for agreement, and take the opening line from your resume's Performance Profile:

"Ten years' experience in office technology sales, including a successful track record selling B-to-B, including corporations, institutions, and small business." You just make it a little less formal and less specific

". . . I'm in office technology sales, with a successful track record selling B-to-B: corporations, institutions, and small business. . . ."

Then complete the spoken version of your Performance Profile. To create a spoken version, take the sentences and turn them into bullet points so that you can't recite the sentences word for word, without sounding like you are reading a script.

Once you have a script, speak it aloud a few times until it sounds conversational and relaxed. Then practice it with a friend or record yourself for critique. Do it in a normal speaking voice until you are comfortable with the content and the rhythm; you'll also know how long it takes. To keep it under the one-minute mark, remember that the idea is just to whet the listener's appetite to know more.

You might take out some information—for example describing yourself as experienced, rather than identifying a specific number of years in your field. This encourages the listener to qualify your statement with a question (How much experience do you have?), and any question denotes a level of interest that might well mean a job exists or is about to exist.

Step 2

Keeping your presentation short and to the point makes Step 2 optional depending on the time you have available and on whether you have something impressive to say about your achievements. If you can cover your Performance Profile points and still have a little time left over, add an example of what you can achieve:

"As the number-three salesperson in my company, I increased sales in my territory fifteen percent, to over one million dollars. In the last six months, I won three major accounts from my competitors—a hospital, a bank, and a technology start-up."

Note that you always talk about what you can do, but never how you do it.

Step 3

Having introduced yourself professionally and succinctly, get to the reason for your call and move the conversation forward.

"The reason I'm calling is that I'm looking for a new challenge, and as I know a little about your company, I felt we might have some areas of common interest. Are these the types of skills and accomplishments you look for in your sales associates?"

Notice that your presentation finishes, not with, "Have you got a job available? Can you hire me?" but with a question that encourages a positive response and opens the possibility of conversation.

When you make your presentation for real, there will likely be a silence on the other end of the line. Be patient, as the employer may need a few seconds to digest your words.

When the employer does respond, it will either be with a question, denoting interest, or with an objection.

Whatever the voice on the other end of the lines says next, try to give short, reasonable answers and finish your reply, when it makes sense to do so, with a question. If a job exists, in answer to your questions the employer will tell you a little about that job. This will define what skills and qualities are important to this employer and help you customize your answers with your most relevant skills and experiences.

Conversation is a two-way street, and you are most likely to win an interview when you take responsibility for your half. Just as the employer's questions show interest in you, your questions should show your interest in the work done at the company. By asking questions of your own in the normal course of conversation—questions usually tagged on to the end of one of your answers—you will forward the conversation.

Here's an example of how such a conversation might proceed. Because you and I come from different backgrounds, we will never talk alike, so with the following sample questions and answers just capture the essence so that you can tailor them to your own speech patterns.

Every word you say has a purpose. Using a common connection gives the person a reason to listen. Mentioning "the courtesy of a few minutes . . ." works because no one wants to be viewed as discourteous. Saying that I don't want a job is code, of course I do but by saying this I take it off the table. If they have a job and we hit it off I won't have to ask.

Ron Weisinger, Principal Development, LINKS Consulting. Human Resources. 20 years' experience.

". . . *The reason I'm calling is that I'm looking for a new challenge, and as I know and respect your product line, I felt we might have areas for discussion. Are these the types of skills and accomplishments you look for in your staff?"*

[Pause]

Miss Shepburn: *"Yes, they are. What type of equipment have you been selling?"* [Buy signal!]

You: *"A comprehensive range from work stations, through routers, modems to printers and ink . . . and all the peripherals you would expect; I sell according to my customers' needs and the capabilities of the technology. I have been noticing a considerable interest in _____ recently. Has that been your experience?"*

Miss Shepburn: *"Yes I have, actually."* [Useful information for you.] *"Do you have a degree?"* [Buy signal!]

You: *"Yes, I do."* [Just enough information to keep the company interested.] *"I understand your company prefers degreed salespeople to deal with its more sophisticated clients."* [Your research is paying off.]

Miss Shepburn: *"Our customer base is very sophisticated, and they expect a certain professionalism and competence from us."* [An inkling of the kind of person the company wants to hire.]*"How much experience do you have?"* [Buy signal!]

You: *"Well, I've worked in both operations and sales, so I understand sales and fulfillment processes, and my customers benefit from not having to deal with false expectations because I understand how to work cooperatively with fulfillment."* [General but thorough.]*"How many years of experience are you looking for?"* [Turning it around, but furthering the conversation.]

Miss Shepburn: *"Ideally, four or five for the position I have in mind."* [More good information.]*"How many do you have?"* [Buy signal!]

You: *"I have two with this company, and one and a half before that, so I fit right in with your needs."*

Miss Shepburn: *"Uh-huh . . . What's your territory?"* [Buy signal!]

You: *"I cover the metropolitan area. Miss Shepburn, it sounds as if we might have something to talk about."* [Remember, your first goal is the face-to-face interview.] *"I am planning to take personal time off next Thursday or Friday. Can we meet then? Which would be best for you?"* [Encourage Miss Shepburn to decide *which* day she can see you, rather than *whether* she will see you.]

Miss Shepburn: *"How about Friday morning?"*

Your questions show interest, carry the conversation forward, and teach you more about the company's needs. By the end of the conversation you have an interview arranged and several key areas you should write down while they are fresh. You can do further research on these areas of interest prior to the interview:

- The company sees growth in _____, so be sure you research what is going on in this particular area.
- They want both professional and personal sophistication.
- They ideally want four or five years' experience.
- They are interested in your metropolitan contacts.

Let's look at the building blocks again before moving on to getting live leads from dead ends:

Step One. Using your Performance Profile as the foundation for all the most pertinent facts, give the employer a succinct verbal snapshot of who you are, and what you bring to the table.

Step Two. Finish your introduction with an example of professional achievements.

Step Three. Move the conversation forward by explaining the reason for your call and finishing with a question that elicits a positive response.

At this point, the employer will either respond with a question or an objection. If it's a question, it shows that the listener is interested. Among the buy signals that often come up are the following:

- "How much experience do you have?" A crucial question, one that you can toss back to the employer: "I have _____ years' chronological experience, but if you could give me a brief outline of the performance requirements I can give you a more accurate answer."

The response will give you a chance to tailor your answer to the employer's requirements.

- "Do you have a degree?" An easy question if you have one. If not, qualify your answer and point the way forward: "My education was cut short by the necessity of earning a living. However, I'm currently enrolled in classes to complete my degree."
- "How much are you making/do you want?" This is delicate, since you don't want to price yourself out of a job. You can ask for more information ("Could you tell me the range for this position?") or give a range; you'll learn how to do this in Chapter 13.

It's extremely important to ask for a face-to-face meeting whenever you have heard and responded to three or more buy signals. Occasionally your calls will go as smoothly as in the example, but not always. This example doesn't show you any number of other tricky questions that, inadequately handled, can rule you out of consideration, or the objections that might be raised and how to handle them. Handling all the buy signals and objections are explored in detail over two chapters in *Knock 'em Dead: The Ultimate Job Search Guide*.

Live Leads from Dead Ends

By no means will every hiring manager you call have a job opening that fits your skills, but you can still turn calls that don't result in interviews into successes. Just a couple of pages back we established that your calls have multiple goals: to arrange an interview, to arrange another time for a conversation, to send a resume for future follow-up, and to develop leads on job openings elsewhere. If there isn't a need for someone like you right now you can ask:

- "When do you anticipate new needs in your area?"
- "May I send you my resume and keep in touch for when the situation changes?"

- "Who else in the company might have a need for someone with my background and skills?"
- "What other companies might have a need for someone with my background?"

If the response is positive:
- "Thanks, I appreciate the help. Do you know who I should speak to?"

If the response to *that* is positive:
- "May I mention your name?"

Mentioning a company you plan to call:
- "Do you know anyone I could speak to at _____?"

If you ask just this sequence of questions you will get leads and introductions, and this enables you to open that next call with:

"Hello, Mr. Jones? My name is Martin Yate, Chuck Harris gave me your name and said to tell you hello. . . ."

but if you don't ask you can never expect to receive. Your call has been entirely professional, and you haven't wasted anyone's time, because the person has either been in your situation or knows it could well happen. You will find the overwhelming majority of people will try to be helpful if you show them a way to do so.

By adding these questions and others in the same vein you will achieve a measure of success from the call, leaving you energized and with a feeling of achievement after every conversation.

Success profile. Treat **everyone** you meet with the same measure of respect/courtesy . . . you never know who you are talking to—and how they may influence a decision to hire you.

Sean Koppelman, President, The Talent Magnet. Advertising, beauty, and entertainment. 16 years' experience.

These are six categories of questions that can lead to job openings, interviews, and offers; read through them and then develop specific questions you can ask in each area:

1. Leads in department
2. Leads in company
3. Leads in other divisions of company
4. Leads to other companies
5. Contacts in other companies
6. Open door to keep in touch

Develop a written list, and keep one on your desktop and one taped by your telephone.

Dealing with Abject Terror

The adrenaline rush you experience when picking up the phone to make the first of these calls is something we associate with fear, and *is normal for anyone engaged in a critical performance activity*. It is a very natural reaction, but because you:

- Know the product you are selling inside out
- Know (from your *TJD* exercises) exactly what you are going to say and how you are going to say it
- Know it will have the greatest relevance and therefore interest to the listener

you will be able to harness the adrenaline rush and channel it into peak performance. Nevertheless, I'd be surprised if you weren't still a little leery at the prospect of calling prospective employers. Three pieces of advice always helped me in my hours of abject terror and I know they will help you too:

- I knew I would never meet these people unless they were interested in what I had to offer, in which case they'd be happy I called.
- Because I was on the phone, no one would know who I was or how scared I felt and looked.
- I knew I had a plan and knew how to make almost every call successful.

It really is pretty easy once you start reaching out and making contact.

> **Successful professionals** change with the technology and are savvy with social networking, just like, "I don't text" wins you nothing, so does "I don't 'friend'" or "I don't tweet."
>
> Olga Ocon, Executive Recruiter, Busch International. VP and CEO-level searches in high-tech. 15 years' experience.

Resources

- *Knock 'em Dead: The Ultimate Job Search Guide*, current annual edition.
- *Knock 'em Dead Cover Letters*, most recent edition.
- For job search letter templates and advice come to *www.knockem dead.com*.

CHAPTER 8

PREPARE TO WIN

You will be asked what you know about the company, so research is necessary if you don't want to underwhelm. You have to choose and prepare a wardrobe that looks professional but not as if you are trying too hard. Most of all, you have to prepare for the interview.

> **What do I need to know about the company?** Most applicants know very little and it shows. Learn as much as you can. Even if you never actually talk about the things you learn, it will help you frame your responses and your questions.
>
> Michelle Hagans, Recruiter, Anu Resources Unlimited. IT and medical. 20+ years' experience.

Become Your Resume

In the time you have between setting the interview and sitting down to answer the first question, and running parallel to your other preparations, you have to become the *professional persona* that you have taken time and effort to capture. You have to become your resume.

Divide your time on a two-to-one ratio. For every hour you spend on the mechanics of preparation, researching the company, your route and means of travel, wardrobe preparation, etc., spend two hours with your resume and preparing for questions. For instance, if it takes two hours to research the company, invest four hours in reviewing everything that went into your resume; if it takes three hours to get your wardrobe together, invest six hours in reviewing interview questions and how you will respond; if it takes an hour to visit the hairdresser, invest two hours in comparing your resume to the job description. By the time you arrive at that job interview, you'll not only *know the stories that go with every line in your resume*, you'll also have complete recall of your professional career and what you bring to the table. You will know how each prioritized responsibility of the job (*TJD*) supports the role it plays within the department and in turn the small role it plays in the complex moneymaking machinery of the company. You will know why that job exists, the problems it is there to *anticipate, prevent, and solve*, and what the holder of this job title needs to do to shine in the role.

This means:

- Take the time to immerse yourself in each of the job's itemized responsibilities, thinking through the many judgment calls you make every day, the *professional values* that help you make those calls correctly, and your logical handling of the challenges and problems that crop up in your work.
- With each of the itemized responsibilities in the *TJD,* you'll have examples of the challenges you've tackled and the successes you've made, sometimes after everything went wrong and all seemed lost; and you'll have instant knowledge of the lessons learned that have helped you grow and become better at your job and more rounded as a professional.
- Consider the specific *transferable skills* that help you execute each aspect of the job. You will have *at least* one example each of how you are developing *technical skills* and one of *transferable skills*.
- Review the behavioral profile for success. In the process, you will consciously identify the *professional values* that inform your actions as you go about your job every day.

- You'll review the profile you identified for *professional failure* in your work.

Time and again you'll go through the job description for this job and your *TJD*, comparing them with the story told in your resume until you can relate *any* item or comment in your *TJD* and your resume to *any* item or comment in the job description. You'll know why each responsibility exists, what it takes to do it well, and how people can screw it up. And as you do so, you'll make an effort to recall the camaraderie and the laughs you had along the way as you lived these experiences, and these memories will help keep your personality alive as you interview, giving depth and dimension to your *professional persona*.

Company Research

> **Be prepared to discuss the company website,** what the company does and how they make their money; review their stock price and its history, and review media coverage of the organization.
>
> Mike Squires, Senior Technical Recruiter, PayPal, an eBay Company.
> 15 years' experience.

The interviewer will expect you to know something about her operations and doesn't want to spend a lot of time explaining what the company does or how it's positioned in the industry. If you cannot answer convincingly it will demonstrate a lack of sincere interest, and you will compare poorly against candidates who make an effort to research the company. If you have done your research, it will show your sincerity and enable you to ask intelligent questions. You should know:

- What the company does, its locations and subsidiaries
- Its current product line and any new products
- News about the company, its products, and key executives
- Its competitors in the industry and in the local market
- Its competitive edge in the market

Visit the company website. Google the company name, brands, products, and/or services, along with the names of any interviewers or other company executives of whom you are aware. Having done this, Google News–search the same terms to find any media coverage.

You can also search your networks and social networking sites for people who work, or have worked, at this company. Learning that you have an interview will encourage most people to give you any insights they can. At the same time, if you know any interviewers' names, search these same social networking sights for their profiles; you won't always find anything, but when you do, it's a nice bonus.

Discover what you can about the position the company occupies within its industry. Is it a leader? Is it growing? How are its products/services distributed? How do these products/services compare to its competitors—in terms of functionality, pricing, and availability?

Your Interview Kit

Put together an interview kit, and when this interview is over you can immediately reassemble it in anticipation of the next one. Your kit will include all the things you'll need to take with you, such as:

- Printed copies of your resume. With electronic resumes now the norm, be sure your interviewers see you in the best possible light, and that is in the layout of the print version of your resume. Take half a dozen copies, so that anyone you meet can have a copy to review. You'll also need a copy for yourself so you can refer to it throughout the interview just as the interviewer refers to it. With everything you have to remember, it can be a very useful frame of reference, *recalling not only what is on the page, but also all the thinking that went into creating it.* Note that it is acceptable to look at your resume when interviewers refer to their copies, but you shouldn't look at it after a question asking for, say, dates of employment and before you answer, because this could imply you don't remember, and some interviewers will question this.

Know your resume. It is shocking how many candidates seem surprised by things that are on their resumes.

Jim Rohan, Senior Partner, J P Canon Associates. Supply chain management. 25 years' experience.

- A folder with a pad of paper and pen. Taking occasional notes shows the interviewer that you're paying attention and that you're organized: A PDA has too many other potential distractions.
- References. Take any reference letters from past employers and/or clients, although they might not be needed and you shouldn't offer them unless requested.

Be prepared. It really astounds me how many people are unprepared to make an impression.

Karen McGrath, PHR. Talent Acquisition Manager, Enterprise Rent-A-Car. 22 years' experience.

- A list of job-related questions. It's good to ask questions during an interview. It shows you're engaged in the discussion and are trying to find out more about how you can integrate yourself into the department and the company.
- If your research generated any interesting articles, print them out and take them along. They indicate your seriousness in researching the company, and sharing them with an interviewer puts the physical proof in their hands.

What do they expect me to know? What they expect isn't important. What's important is that you exceed their expectations. Study their competitors and ask questions accordingly: "I see that your competitor _____ has released a new product. How will you compete with that?" Or "I heard that _____ has filed for bankruptcy. Is that an opportunity for you to pick up market share?"

Rich Gold, CPC. Smith Arnold Partners. Finance recruiter. 20 years' experience.

- Directions to the interview, including different means of transportation and a time frame for travel. Nothing is worse than getting lost and being late to a job interview. Way before you depart—you should *never* leave this till the last minute—determine the interview location (building floor, street address, telephone numbers), what transportation you'll use, and the time needed for travel. Murphy's Law tells you that everything that can go wrong will go wrong on such an important day, so anticipate this and allow plenty of extra time for traffic delays. Getting to the location of the interview with *plenty of time to spare* is the only way you can guarantee showing up at the interview calm, punctual, and ready for battle.

Dress and Grooming

Dress. When you walk in the room, they are evaluating you as a client or customer would; and often making a quick decision about your fit with the organization, based on your appearance and manner.

Denise Wilkerson, RN, CPC. Executive Search Director, Global Edge Recruiting. Medical devices, biotech, pharma, sales/marketing management. 14+ years' experience.

Business dress for both men and women has slowly been changing and today there's a much wider range of acceptable clothing in the workplace. Nevertheless, even if a company is relatively casual in its everyday dress code, your appearance needs to show that you understand what constitutes professional dress. It shows respect for the occasion and the interviewer, and that you know what to wear when representing the company. Looking your best also helps your self-confidence, and that sends positive messages to your interviewers. Your goal is to *cause the least amount of possible offense to the greatest number of people*, so if in doubt lean toward the clean-cut and conservative.

Men's Clothing

How should I dress? This is what I do for a living, and I'm telling you it's better to be the only person in the room dressed formally, than the only person NOT.

Paul Cameron, President, DriveStaff Inc. Technology recruitment.
14 years' experience.

You know the dress code for your profession and industry, and that will help you personalize this advice. If suits are the norm, wear a suit, navy and gray being the safest choices; if not, a jacket and tie. Even if day-to-day dress is very casual, interviewers need to know that you understand professional dress codes for when they are necessary; and they are pleased when you remove the doubt. The higher your professional level and pay grade and the more your job requires you to interact with company clients or others at the top of the socio-economic food chain, the more care you must give to the protocols of professional dress. For shirts, wear a long-sleeve white or pale blue shirt. White shirts always look sharp and transmit messages of honesty, intelligence, and stability. Cotton shirts look best and show perspiration less. For shoes, wear black or brown, and they must be polished; your socks should match the color of your trousers.

Avoid chains, medallions, earrings, and Mickey Mouse wrist-watches, and if you have tattoos, cover them up. A briefcase helps create a professional image and it gives you a good place to carry everything you need to take, including a hairbrush and a cotton handkerchief or something similar to wipe your hands with before meeting the interviewer so you avoid those delightful cold and sweaty palms that always come with job interviews.

Use deodorant, but don't use cologne; there isn't a man in the world who knows when to stop, and overwhelming your audience with aromas primarily developed to increase sexual attractiveness is not the right message for your interview.

Women's Clothing

How should I dress? Dress like you want the job, not like you already have it! However, if you are twenty-two years old—you are not expected to look like you are fifty-two years old. Certain industries require a balance of professional—yet fashionable.

Sean Koppelman, President, The Talent Magnet. Advertising, beauty, and entertainment. 16 years' experience.

Women have a wider variety of business clothing options available to them than men, and a hundred more issues that increase the possibility of missteps. As with men, the first and last guiding principle is that you are trying to get hired, not dated. This is especially important to women intent on climbing the professional ladder alongside their male colleagues. Fashion has much greater impact on dress for women, but you cannot take your professional dress advice from women's magazines, because they exist to sell this season's fashions. The rule of thumb is that your appearance should complement, not detract from, the professional message you want to convey.

Dress considerations should include:

- Your skirt length. Regardless of fashion standards, remember the rule: *least offense to the greatest number of people.* This means lean toward conservative—never more than two inches above the knee is a good guideline. Nothing too tight or with slits.
- Whether or not you are wearing a suit, long sleeves are the most professional look. Displaying cleavage is unwise, and skin-tight is not a smart idea. Plain or striped is good, patterns not so much. Cotton always looks professional and is good at concealing nervous perspiration stains.
- Jewelry is acceptable, but less is usually more effective. Steer away from long or hoop earrings.
- Your shoes should be coordinated with the rest of your outfit. Stay away from platforms, and heels over two-and-a-half to three inches. Anything taller will make you look wobbly and unprofessional.

- Pantyhose should be in a neutral skin color and should not be patterned.
- Take a briefcase but not a shoulder bag as well. Put what you need in a clutch and the clutch inside a briefcase: It's less to juggle and gives you a sleeker, more business-like appearance.
- There's a difference between daytime and evening makeup; even if an interview includes dinner, wear daytime makeup. Wear less jewelry than you would normally, and tone down any tendency toward creative nail decoration.

General Grooming

Interviews are nervous affairs, and the nerves start kicking in up to twenty-four hours before the event. Shower, accompanied by unscented deodorants and antiperspirants. Stay away from spicy foods, onions, garlic, and alcohol for a couple of days before an interview, and pay attention to teeth and breath. For men . . . remember that eyebrow, nose, and ear hair grow stronger and wilder with age.

The Final Package

Ask good questions. The questions you ask at an interview can be more impressive than the statements on your resume.

Nancy C. Anton, CPC. Talent Consultant, CIGNA. 20 years' experience.

The less baggage you have to deal with the better, but these items all have a place in your briefcase:

- A cell/PDA with the interviewer's office and mobile contact information
- Copies of your resume and perhaps executive briefing
- A list of job-related questions
- Laptop
- A hairbrush or comb

- A spare pair of tights (you can skip this item if you're a guy)
- Bottled water

Always include a couple of Power Bars or other non-sugar-high sustenance; you need to have good blood sugar levels to help you maintain peak performance. Eat one thirty minutes before the interview. If lunch or dinner is on the schedule, it's not a bad idea to eat one right before. You are at those meals to sell yourself: Talking, not eating, is the main item on the menu.

First Impressions

The interview begins with your initial meeting with the interviewer. Although jobs can be won or lost at any point during an interview, it's also true that you can lose a job because of first impressions. Fortunately it is fairly easy to avoid making a bad impression and get your interview off to a good start.

The key to success here is *body language*. It is said that more than half of all effective communication depends on *body language*, because it's our oldest form of communication, and carries enormous weight in the subconscious.

Shake Hands
Let the interviewer initiate the handshake. Match the pressure and style of her shake; it's brief, maybe 1–2 seconds. At the end of the interview, follow and mirror your interviewer's lead.

Personal Space
Whether standing or sitting, we all have a personal space that it is wisest not to invade. A thirty-inch zone surrounding the other person is widely perceived to be everyone's comfort zone. Stay standing until you're invited to sit.

When standing: Keep your posture erect; don't put your hands in your pockets, and don't hook your fingers into your belt.

When sitting: Once you've been offered a seat, avoid nervous fiddling. That's why it's a good idea to take a folder and pen. Keep your back against the back of the chair: It keeps you looking alert and helps you avoid slouching, which many of us do when we are feeling nervous.

Look at the Interviewer

During the interview you want to show that you're interested in what's being said. Look at the interviewer while he is talking. You should smile or nod from time to time to show that you understand and are interested in what is being said; you can also make the occasional appreciative murmur to communicate the same thing. When you are nervous it is easy to forget to smile, and your smile shows friendliness and engagement in what is being said.

Barricades

Avoid sending negative signals during the interview. Crossing your arms sends signals that you are feeling defensive and can suggest that you're hiding something or are defiant. If you cross your legs with an ankle over the other knee, this sends the same negative signal.

Last of the Small Talk

As you and the interviewer get settled in your seats the last of the small talk is being exchanged. Depending on the job, part of this ritual can be the exchange of business cards; you are not expected to have a card if you are between jobs. Now, before the questions start flying, we are going to take a look inside the hiring manager's mind.

CHAPTER 9

THE FIVE SECRETS OF THE HIRE

There are five secrets to acing a job interview. These secrets are based on the logical evaluations that interviewers make when hiring for any job, at any level and in every profession. Understanding them will help you beyond learning how to turn job interviews into job offers; they will show you ways to become more successful on your next job and throughout your career.

The five secrets will give you further evidence that the *transferable skills* and *professional values* are of importance to a successful career. Their presence in your portfolio of skills can turn interviews into offers and your next job and the balance of your career into a greater success story. Understand these five secrets and you'll have a huge advantage in distinguishing yourself from other candidates and landing the job.

The First Secret: Ability and Suitability

You have to show a clear grasp of the job and the role it plays in the department and as a small but important cog in the complex moneymaking machinery of the corporation. You must demonstrate an *ability* to do the work; that you are in full possession of the *technical skills* required for skillful execution of your responsibilities and that you know how to use them.

> **Transferable skills.** Every job worth having requires problem-solving skills. Without them, success is elusive.
>
> Don Orlando, MBA, CPRW, JCTC. Owner, The McLean Group. Coaching senior executives. 17 years' experience.

You must also establish your *suitability* for the job. This includes appearance, demeanor, and the sense of unforced professional competency you project. Of equal importance is that you understand the protocols and speak the language of your profession.

For example, a computer programmer working in a bank has *technical skills*. She shows *ability* to do the job by demonstrating possession of the skills and how to apply them in writing good code. She shows *suitability* for the job by demonstrating an understanding of how the program will be used in application and why it will be used that way. That comes from a *familiarity with the operations of the world of banking and finance and its terminology.*

But wait, you say, a computer programmer doesn't have to know banking: She can pick that up fairly quickly. It's the programming skills that are important. I don't disagree, but if you were hiring and you had to pick between two programmers with equal technical skills, who would *you* hire, the one who knew your business or the one who didn't?

Given the transferability of certain *technical skills*, suitability is one of the biggest hurdles career-changers have to overcome in both their resumes and in the ensuing interviews. If you are considering a career change, you can use understanding of this first secret of the hire as part of your preparation to make that career change. Take time to find people already doing this work in your target industry/profession who can explain the mechanics of the business and the reasons for those mechanics, the professional protocols that have been developed to deal with the realities and contingencies of that world, and the language professionals in the field use to discuss them, so that in turn you can make the connections between your credentials and the new world in which they will be applied.

The Second Secret:
Every Job Is about Problem Resolution

They are looking for someone to solve their problems and make their lives easier.

Eric Kramer, Chief Innovation Officer, Innovative Career Services. Psychologist, career and interview coaching. 10 years' experience.

Regardless of profession or job title, the only reason your job exists is to help the company generate revenue. Being aware of this is absolutely vital to job search and career success in any field. Explain to an interviewer that you understand *your job is to anticipate, prevent, and solve the problems within your area of authority*, and can back it up in conversation: Bells will ring; indeed, the poor old dear might drop dead and go to heaven on the spot.

Backing this up in conversation brings us to a reminder of the importance of *critical thinking*. Once you have identified the particular problem-solving business you are in, you've gone a long way toward isolating what the interviewer will want to talk about. The *TJD* exercises helped you identify the typical problems that are the meat and potatoes of your work and gave you plenty of examples of your use of *critical thinking* skills. When you can tell stories of problems you've dealt with efficiently, it helps interviewers visualize you solving their problems—on their payroll, as a member of the team.

There are two benefits to this. You demonstrate a professional awareness that is part of the behavioral profile of a high-achiever, and you can leverage your advantage by turning a one-sided examination of skills into a two-way conversation between a couple of professionals with a common interest: You can ask questions about the guts of the job, its problems, challenges, projects, and deadlines, and the pressure points that need to be tackled. This is important because interviewers evaluate candidates not only on what they say but on the questions they ask, because the *questions demonstrate the depth of that candidate's understanding*. Other candidates won't be able to do this, let alone follow up on the interviewer's answers by illustrating how they can hit the ground running on those critical projects.

The Third Secret: Professionals Are Professional Because They *Behave* That Way

Transferable skills? Extremely important. Indicated through examples of how you do your work, rather than saying, "I'm a great _____."

Glenna Cose Brin, CPC. President, Alliance Staff. High-end administration. 30+ years' experience.

Becoming a professional in your field means your behavior is perceived as professional. It is your embodiment of the *transferable skills* and *professional values* that does most to convey this message. They inform your judgments, opinions, and conduct in everything you do.

An important component of your interview arsenal is the ability to show employers you are in possession of the full slate of these universally sought *transferable skills*. Exhibiting the *transferable skills* in action as well as in your response to questions gives your answers substance and the ring of truth. Along with the other four secrets of the hire, they are your passport to success at any interview.

The Fourth Secret: Motivation and Intelligent Enthusiasm

How should I behave? Be a slightly more energetic version of yourself in an interview. Smile—convey happiness about where you are and excitement about the possibilities this job may offer.

Sean Koppelman, President, The Talent Magnet. Advertising, beauty, and entertainment. 16 years' experience.

Motivation is one of the *professional values* we identified as something all employers love to see in their employees. From the employer's side of the desk, the thinking behind a preference for motivated, *intelligently enthusiastic* candidates is roughly this:

- The more motivated professional and more *intelligently enthusiastic* candidate will work harder and will turn in a better work product.
- Someone who really enjoys his work and is engaged in his profession will show that it is going to be easy to work with him, and that he will be a positive influence and a welcome, happy addition to the team.
- Someone who is enthusiastic and motivated by his work is likely to have a greater commitment to take the rough with the smooth. In a tightly run job race, when there is really nothing to choose between two top contenders, the job offer will always go to the most *intelligently enthusiastic* candidate.

This is an important consideration, because interviews are uncomfortable and often stressful situations for anyone. When you are uncomfortable or stressed, your defenses are up and you retreat behind a wall of stiff formality, and the natural enthusiasm and motivations that are normally part of your *professional persona* are restrained.

So, the fourth secret of the hire is to allow your natural enthusiasm for your work and for this job opportunity to shine through, rather than hide it because of interview nerves or a misconstrued sense of professionalism.

The one thing that can be a deal breaker: Attitude. The right attitude is everything.

Nancy C. Anton, CPC. Talent Consultant, CIGNA. 20 years' experience.

When it comes to a tightly run job race between equally qualified candidates, remember that *the offer will always go to the most* intelligently enthusiastic *candidate*. Show your enthusiasm for the job and make it clear that you are excited about the opportunity to become a member of this team. Your visible motivation can tip the scales in your favor.

The Fifth Secret: Teamwork and Manageability

Teamwork, the ability to function productively as a member of a group focused on achieving goals that exceed the scope of any single job, is another of the *transferable skills*. This ability to function as an integrated member of a team that on occasion exceeds the confines of your immediate department team is important, since so many of the contributions a department makes toward the smooth running of the corporate machinery are crucially important and far beyond the scope of individual contribution.

Working on a team takes patience, balance, tolerance, and an ability to assert your own personality without overpowering everyone else's; it requires *emotional intelligence*. Remember: You don't have to *like* everyone on your team, but you have to be able to *work* with them, and that requires *emotional maturity*.

When you embrace and apply the five secrets, you will win job offers and keeping them in mind on your new job will increase your credibility, the speed of your acceptance by management and your peers, and will support your career journey, wherever it might lead you.

CHAPTER 10

MEET YOUR INTERVIEWERS: WHY THEY DO THE THINGS THEY DO

Sitting in front of the interviewer, your mind racing with the possibilities of what could happen next as he looks over your resume, you are probably thinking, "This is crazy. Why am I here? I'd rather be abducted by aliens." What probably won't occur to you is that quite a lot of the time the interviewer feels the same way.

How Interviews Are Organized

Interviewers come in two flavors:

1. The experienced interviewer knows what she is doing and has a plan for the interview.
2. The inexperienced interviewer doesn't know what he is doing, and worse, *doesn't know* he doesn't know what he is doing; he's what's known as an unconscious incompetent.

Good questions to ask an unconscious incompetent. What is a typical day? What will I have done six months from now to be successful in this job? This gets the interviewer to talk about what they want and will give the candidate insights for comparison of skills to the company's needs.

Maynard G. Charron, President, Paper Industry Recruitment. 30+ years' experience.

The Experienced Interviewer

A manager's job is to get work done through others, and the first step is to hire the right people; because if you cannot hire effectively, you can never manage productively; and if you can't manage productively . . . you lose your job. Consequently, most managers learn how to interview effectively. You can also rely on just about all headhunters, corporate recruiters, and HR people to run competent interviews because it's what they do every day.

Competent interviewers have a plan, they know what they are going to ask, why they are asking it, what they hope to find, and when they are going to ask it. They have all been in many more interviews than you have. Three pointers we can gain from this:

- They can tell fact from fiction and truth from dreams. You don't need to exaggerate or fabricate: What you have to say is going to capture their full attention.
- Interviewing can get boring if you do a lot of it. The majority of candidates make this worse. You don't need to be uptight or stiff; try to relax and become the friendly, competent, outgoing person you are on your best days. Just don't be a wise-ass.
- This is a job: It needs to be completed so they can go on to the next one. Your interviewers are hoping, praying, that you will be the one.

Competent interviewers always have a plan for the interview, and this is what it looks like from the other side of the desk:

How interviews are organized

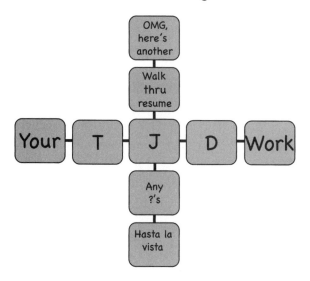

"OMG, Here's Another One."

Yes, that's the first thought in the interviewer's mind as you sit down to begin the interview. It continues, "I pray to the baby Jesus that this is the one. All I want is someone who 'gets' the job, can do it and wants to do it, comes to work on a regular basis, and gets on with people. I just need to hire someone and get on to the next project!"

> **How do they think?** Can this person do the job and will need minimal ramp-up time? Will s/he fit with the team? Can s/he handle the supervision of _____? Will I be looking for a replacement in six months because they've left? Are they looking for advancement right away, leaving me to look for a replacement in six months?
>
> Michelle Hagans, Recruiter, Anu Resources Unlimited. IT and medical. 20+ years' experience.

Contrary to what you may think, *the interviewer wants you to relax*. That's because a more relaxed you is a more communicative you, and the interviewer wants lots of information on which to base his decision. So at the beginning of any interview you'll move through some formulaic small talk and the offer of a beverage to prepare the way for the actual questioning to begin. Always accept the beverage, and ask for water. You *are* nervous, your throat is more prone to dryness, and water is the best remedy.

The interview gets underway with a statement from the interviewer, who will say something along the lines of, "We're looking for a _____, and I want to find out about your experience and the strengths you can bring to our team." She will then explain a bit about how the interview itself will go: whether you'll be talking to other people and if so, who they are. This is the time when you offer a nicely formatted version of your resume printed on decent paper, because next the interviewer is going to glance down at the resume, and say, "So tell me a little bit about yourself. . . ."

Walk Through Your Resume

> **What kills an interview?** Not listening, interrupting me when I'm speaking or trying to say something when I haven't finished my thought, and the worst, overconfidence.
>
> Karen McGrath, PHR. Talent Acquisition Manager, Enterprise Rent-A-Car. 22 years' experience.

Using your resume as a referral document, interviewers typically walk through your work history, asking you questions about different aspects of your experience. These early questions are designed to get you comfortable with talking, so they will mostly be straightforward, since a good interviewer wants to limit his contributions to about 20 percent of the interview, leaving you to talk the other 80 percent of the time—offering plenty of time to analyze your answers. Your answers should be similarly straightforward, and you'll make an effort here to show an understanding, in general terms, of your job's role within the department. You'll show you know that in essence the job is *problem identification, prevention, and solution.*

Some interviews end after this journey through the resume, either because the interviewer has enough information to rule you out, or because he doesn't know any better. Skilled interviewers use this walk through the resume as a qualifying round. If you pass, they'll take the interview to the next level.

Your *TJD* Work Pays Off

They quickly determine if you can "walk and chew gum." Then they drill down into your accomplishments, especially the "how."

Ron Weisinger, Principal Development, LINKS Consulting. Human Resources. 20 years' experience.

Now the interviewer wants to look at your qualifications and experience in each of the critical deliverables of the job. Your resume was based on the focus you gained from *TJD*: Its Performance Profile captured your qualifications in exactly these critical deliverables, and the Core Competencies section backed this up with headlines on the relevant skills and experiences. You also invested time in researching the company and in working back and forth between the Job Description, the *TJD*, and your resume, connecting experiences to the *problems anticipated, prevented, and solved* in each area by application of your *technical* and *transferable skills*: You can connect any topic the interviewer raises to the qualifications you bring to the table and illustrate it with real-world examples, explaining what you did and why you did it, the underlying skills you used to get it done and the values that helped you make the right judgment calls, and finally what you learned and how you grew professionally from the experience. The first questions will deal with the most important deliverables of the job, and gradually the discussion will shift to those areas that are less important, though nice to have.

Any Questions?

You know the interview is drawing to a close when you are asked if you have any questions. In Chapter 8, I suggested you make a list of such questions. Bringing the list out and checking off what hasn't been covered demonstrates the kind of *intelligent enthusiasm* that, again, helps set you apart from other candidates. The list you develop for your first interview can be the template for all subsequent interviews.

Hasta la Vista, Baby

The interviewer will thank you for your time and may give you some idea of next steps. If this information isn't offered, ask for it. If there is another round of interviews:

- Recap your understanding of the job
- Recap what you bring to the table
- Restate that you are qualified and very interested
- Ask to schedule the next interview

If there are no more interviews, ask when the decision will be made. Then repeat the steps above, but instead of asking for the next interview, ask for the job. You have everything to gain and nothing to lose; showing motivation and *intelligent enthusiasm* for the job now could be the decisive factor.

Interview Strategies

Although all interviews will follow a schematic similar to the one above, there are a number of strategies that interviewers use either singly or in combination to get to the truth.

1. Stress
2. Behavioral
3. Situational

We'll look at them in order.

Stress Strategies

Any job interview is a stress interview. Beyond that, if the ability to function under stress is part of your job—for example, sales—then some aspects of the interview might try to create a little stress. Interviewers usually don't see it as stress, they just want to see if you can handle the tough questions.

Whenever you feel stress in an interview, stay calm:

- Breathe evenly and calmly. Shortness of breath will inhibit your thinking process and make you sound nervous.
- If you've been offered a glass of water, take a sip. It buys you time and swallowing reduces the tension a little and gets the frog out of your throat (there are more techniques to gain time later in this chapter).
- Keep your body posture relaxed and open. Many people have a tendency, when under stress, to contract their bodies. This adds to the tension and sends the wrong message.
- Think through the question. Consciously remove any real or perceived intimidating verbal inflection. For example, depending on the tone of voice used, the question, "I'm not sure you are right for the job. What do you think?" can be heard as, "You just aren't right for this job." With a different tone, it may come across as, "I'd like to hire you and you're one of my top candidates, but I'm not sure you're the one, so please convince me."

Who gets hired? Positive and likable people get hired.

Perry Newman, CPC/CSMS. Executive Resume Writer/Career Coach. 25 years' experience.

Behavioral Interview Strategies

Behavioral interviewing has become an integral part of almost every interview. This approach is based on the reasonable premise that your past behavior predicts your future performance: "If I know how you behaved on someone else's payroll, I'll know how you will behave on mine." The interviewer asks a general question about a skill area and then asks you to talk about specific events. "Tell me about a time when. . . ."

Behavioral interviewing also looks for balance. If the interviewer is feeling impressed, she will try to temper a positive response with, "Great, now tell me about a time when things didn't work out so well." You are ready, because you also came up with examples that answer this, examples that show you redeeming the situation or learning a valuable lesson from it.

Situational Strategies

Situational strategies give the interviewer an opportunity to see you in something close to a real-world situation, in the belief that he will have a better idea of how you perform your duties. The situational strategy will always relate to a frequently executed task, something at the very heart of your job, and it can happen as a formal part of the interview or very casually.

Customer service and sales jobs are prone to situational interviewing strategies more than most; if you face one of these, you'll panic a little, but the situational role play is going to recreate a task or situation that is at the core of your work. Ask a few questions for clarification and to get nerves under control. If it's going to take more than a few minutes you can ask for a restroom break. Then, as much as you can, relax, step up, and do your job. Remember, what is being sought is confirmation that you understand the building blocks of that task: You aren't expected to deliver an Oscar-worthy performance.

Tell success stories. When you explain how you make things happen, interviewers can picture you doing the same things for them. Follow a "Challenge—Actions—Results" framework to illustrate your examples.

Meg Guiseppi, C-level Executive Job Search Coach, Executive Career Brand. 20+ years' experience.

Keeping Up Your End of the Conversation

There are a number of techniques you can use to keep up your end of the conversation: tactics to clarify questions, buy time to think, and ask useful questions of your own.

1. You can show engagement with what the interviewer is saying by giving verbal signals; you do this with occasional short, quiet interjections that don't interrupt the employer's flow but let him know you are paying attention: "Uh-huh," "that's interesting," "okay," "great," and "yes, yes" all work; but be careful not to overdo it.
2. You can use the question strategies that interviewers use.
3. If you don't fully understand a question, or if you need time to think, ask, "Would you run that by me again?" The question is not only repeated, it is usually repeated with more detail, giving additional information and time to formulate an answer.
4. If a question stumps you, and having it repeated still doesn't help, it is better to say, "I'd like to come back to that later, I'm not used to interviewing and I'm nervous and drawing a blank right now." Odds are the interviewer will forget to ask again; if she remembers, at least your mind will have been working on it in the background, and with the extra time will probably come up with an answer. If you have a great answer and the interviewer doesn't bring it up again, you can.
5. When you want to make a point and the interviewer isn't asking questions that allow you to make it, ask questions like these, "Would it be of value if I described my experience with _____?" or "Then my experience in _____ should be a great help to you" or "I recently completed an accounting project just like that. Would it be relevant to discuss it?"

Success? Right attitude, fresh, curious, happy to help others, in touch with what is going on, a value of information and ideas, with the follow through that most lack. Up-to-date on technology and uses it, with ease.

Nancy C. Anton, CPC. Talent Consultant, CIGNA. 20 years' experience.

Conversation Etiquette

Speak clearly and be careful not to mumble or shout, either of which can happen when you are nervous.

1. If you find your throat gets dry, stop and take a drink of water. The interviewer will be patient.
2. If for any reason you become flustered, stop for a moment and collect your thoughts before continuing. It's better to take a few seconds to calm down than to dig a hole deeper and deeper with babbling.
3. Keep in mind that the 80/20 rule applies to you as well. It's all right to talk a lot—that's what the interviewer expects—but don't dominate the conversation to the exclusion of anyone else. If the interviewer signals that he wants to communicate something, let him do so.
4. *Never* interrupt. You want all information possible before engaging your mouth.

Who gets hired? Someone who is assertive without being arrogant or verbose, but who can articulate quantifiable achievements and experience, will most often get the job.

Joe Murawski, CPC. Executive Search Consultant, Focused Hire. Aerospace, defense, and high-tech electronics. 15 years' experience.

Information-Gathering Questions

Demonstrate a good understanding of the job's deliverables and your possession of all the *technical* and *transferable skills* and *professional values* that help you do the job well, and you will be a top contender. Learn to turn a one-sided examination of skills into a two-way conversation between professionals with a common interest.

1. Don't be afraid to ask questions. Your questions show interest, and we make our judgments of people based on both the statements they make and the questions they ask. The questions you ask show that you get the job and take it seriously. The interviewer's answers deliver insights into the job that you wouldn't otherwise have, giving you a better focus for your responses and the points you want to make.

   This is especially important when the interviewer does not give you the openings you need to sell yourself. Always have a few intelligent questions prepared to save the situation. The following questions will give you an excellent idea of why the position is open and exactly the kind of skilled professional the company will eventually hire:

- "Who succeeds in this job and why?"
- "Who fails in this job and why?"
- "What do you consider the most important day-to-day responsibilities of this job?"
- "What is the hardest part of the job?"
- "What will be the first projects I tackle?"
- "What will you want me to have achieved in the first ninety days?"
- "What are the biggest challenges the department faces this year and what will be my role as a team member in tackling them?"
- "Which projects will I be most involved with during the first six months?"

- "What will you want me to have achieved in the first six months?"
- "What are the challenges you are facing in this area?"
- "What personality traits do you consider critical to success in this job?"

2. When you get a clear understanding of an employer's needs with questions like these, you can seize the opportunity to sell yourself appropriately, using the same techniques you would use when an interviewer talks but doesn't ask questions. Using that list as a starting point, make a list of your own to take to your job interviews.

You need to have the right focus going into the interview. *You are not going to the interview to decide if you want the job,* because you have nothing to decide until an offer is on the table. You are at the interview for one reason only: to get a job offer. Nothing else matters. Turning interviews into job offers is a critical professional survival skill, yet *of all the professional skills you possess, this one is the weakest.* When you focus your interview performance on getting job offers, you will turn a critical weakness into an invaluable strength.

Resources

Panel interviews, role play, and inbox tests are addressed in the latest annual edition of *Knock 'em Dead: The Ultimate Job Search Guide.*

CHAPTER 11

KNOCK 'EM DEAD AT THE INTERVIEW

There are no magical answers to an interviewer's questions, but with an understanding of what's behind them, what you have to offer, and an understanding of how and why the professional world works the way it does, you can be prepared with answers that are genuine and honest, *and* advance your candidacy. Even *before* we go through the question/response strategies of this chapter you are well prepared. Your *TJD* exercises tell you how employers think about the responsibilities of this job:

- How they prioritize its needs
- The words they use to think about and describe it

You went through your work experience and developed:

- Examples of *identifying, preventing, and solving problems* in each of the job's areas of responsibility
- Examples of how each of the *transferable skills* helps you execute each of the job's responsibilities
- A profile for successful behavior backed by an understanding of the *professional values* that underlie such behavior

You're ready to show them a genuine grasp of the work, plus you will be able to illustrate your answers with examples that show *how you are able* to do the things you do. Your resume reflects these abilities and tells a compelling story about your qualifications for this job. This means that before the job interview, the interviewer is well disposed toward you.

Is it possible to talk too much in an interview? An interview is a sales call. You should never be "too" anything. The mission is to get an offer, not to get a laugh or get [money/benefit] questions answered. There will be time to get questions answered after the offer.

Jim Rohan, Senior Partner, J P Canon Associates. Supply chain management. 25 years' experience.

Now we are going to examine some of the toughest questions that can come your way, and learn the tactics that will help you deliver great and honest answers to these tough questions and turn job interviews into job offers.

The suggested approaches to these tough questions aren't written to give you slick answers. They're written to increase your *real* understanding of how and why the professional world works the way it does, and so help you create personal answers that will resonate with the ring of truth. The toughest questions obviously vary from person to person and depend on individual circumstances, but the ones we handle in this chapter are frequently asked questions that can trip anyone up.

What gets an interview off on the right foot? A great smile, handshake, introduction, good eye contact, being appropriately dressed and knowing your stuff.

Bill Wilhelm, CPC. Executive Search Director, Wilhelm and Associates, Inc. Industrial Sales and Manufacturing Management. 38 years' experience.

Tell me a little about yourself.

There's logic behind the question: The interviewer knows you are nervous and that talking will help you relax. Simultaneously he wants to know about your experience and qualifications for this job, and if they warrant you being here. Answer the question well and you create a good first impression and set the tone for your candidacy; you also immediately feel more confident.

You already have the answer to this question prepared:

- Doing your *TJD* exercise helped you determine how employers prioritize the deliverables of this job.
- Your resume developed all the relevant experience you needed in each of these areas to tell the best story.
- The Performance Profile that kicks off your resume encapsulated all the most crucial experience in a few short sentences.

Your answer to this question takes the essence of your Performance Profile and turns it back into full sentences, giving you a condensed professional work history that focuses on the most important experience. Add chronology—"I spent _____ years at _____ and this is where I learned _____"—and you'll show the professional development that brought you to where you are today.

> **What gets an interview off on the right foot?** I have heard often it is how you answer the **"Tell me about yourself"** question and I believe this is true.
>
> Denise Wilkerson, RN, CPC. Executive Search Director, Global Edge Recruiting. Medical devices, biotech, pharma, sales/marketing management. 14+ years' experience.

What do you know about the company?

The interviewer spends the majority of her waking hours in the environment that the winning candidate will join. Your knowledge of the job and the company is a piece of the jigsaw puzzle that helps the interviewer evaluate your enthusiasm and motivation for your work.

If you don't understand what the company does and is known for you will lose out to candidates who do.

Use the Internet, company website, and networking contacts to give you insight into the company, its products, and why it is a good place to work. You need to visit the company website and read media coverage on the company and its key executives (by searching Google News), as well as general news about the issues affecting your profession. Your research will raise as many questions as it answers, and you can use this in your answer: "I read that _____, and wonder how this is affecting you. . . ?" Such questions demonstrate engagement with your profession and get the interviewer talking, perhaps giving you useful information. It's okay to throw in some personal details as well, such as the fact that working for the company will bring you closer to family.

Walk me through your job changes.

This question comes early in an interview and helps the interviewer understand the chronology and reasoning behind your career moves and gaps in employment. Don't worry about gaps; everyone has to deal with them. You must be ready to walk through your resume, without hesitation, making two statements about each employer:

1. What you learned from that job that applies to this one
2. Why you left

Relate the example of experience from each company to the needs of the job for which you are interviewing.

Why did you leave _____ company?

This is a checkbox question—the interviewer wants to ask the question, check the box, and move on. You get into trouble with too much information. Any answer longer than fifteen words is too long; if the interviewer wants more, she will ask.

Acceptable reasons for leaving a job: job not as described; company in financial difficulties; downsized; declined to relocate; too many changes (management, pay plans, direction); underpaid; incentives eliminated; limited or no growth.

Acceptable reasons for leaving sales jobs: quota raised; territory shrunk/changed; accounts taken away; commission changed; unpaid commissions; product doesn't work/overpriced/ noncompetitive.

Bob Morris. Owner, Storage Placements. Data storage sales/marketing. 44 years' experience.

Why have you changed jobs so frequently?

If you have jumped around, blame it on getting caught in layoffs during recessions or youth. Hopefully, you can explain that it was never as a result of poor performance and that you grew professionally as a result of each job change.

Your answer should be short; dwelling on the situation only makes interviewers probe for more. You may be able to explain how this broad experience has helped you open up to new ideas and ways of doing things, or to how truly valuable *teamwork* and good management are.

Emphasize that and why you are more settled now. For example, if you blame your frequent job changes on youth (even the interviewer was young once), explain that you realize what a mistake your job-hopping was, and that with your added domestic responsibilities you are much more settled now. Whatever the case, carefully think out your reasons for leaving each job in advance of the interview.

Listen to the question. The most important information in a sentence is in the second half. Bright people tend to speak quickly and start formulating an answer before really hearing the entire sentence. LISTEN CAREFULLY! Pause before you comment and make sure you have heard the entire question.

Marjean Bean, CPC. President, Medit Staff. Information technology. 30+ years' experience.

Why were you fired?

Don't mistake getting laid off with being terminated for cause. If you were fired and you don't try to clean up the mess *and* change your ways, it can dog you for years.

Firing someone is unpleasant and never a decision any manager makes lightly.

The first and most important thing you must do is take responsibility for the actions or behavior that led to your dismissal, because 99 times out of 100 the responsibility lies at your door. If you do not take responsibility for your actions, you cannot change them, and the problems that led to you getting fired will repeat themselves, quite possibly destroying the promise of your career.

If you take responsibility for your actions, you can clean up your act and clean up the past. Call the person who fired you; your aim is to clear the air, so whatever you do, don't be antagonistic. Reintroduce yourself and explain that you are looking (or, if you have been unemployed for a while, say you are "still looking") for a new job. Say that you appreciate that the manager had to do what was done, *that you want to apologize for being such a problem*, that you learned from the experience, and exactly what you learned that has helped you become a more responsible professional.

Then ask, "If you were asked as part of a pre- or post-employment reference check, what would you say about me? How would you describe my leaving the company? Would you say that I was fired or that I simply resigned? You see, every time I tell someone about my termination, whoosh, there goes another chance of getting back to work!"

If you apologize and demonstrate that you have changed, often that manager will plump for the latter option (describing your departure as a resignation). Taking responsibility and cleaning up the past really works and is the first step in putting yourself back on a successful track.

If you take this approach, maybe you'll even be able to finish, "My boss and I are on good terms these days. He'll confirm what I've told you and in fact will give me a decent reference."

Have you ever been asked to resign?

When someone is asked to resign, it is a gesture on the part of the employer: "You can quit, or we will can you, so which do you want it to be?" Because you were given the option, though, the employer cannot later say, "I had to ask him to resign"—that is tantamount to firing and could lead to legal problems. If you answer, "Yes," it's a mark against you and can derail your candidacy, so in the final analysis, it is safe to answer, "No."

Why does your resume have a gap? Or *Why were you out of work so long?*

Whatever the reason for your hiatus, be honest. Discuss the decisions behind your absence from the workplace, whatever they were. *What's most important to the interviewer is if and how long it will take you to be productive if hired.*

Your answer should emphasize that while you may not have been in the corporate workplace, you have certainly not been idle. Talk about how you have kept current with classes or part-time work, and/or what you have been doing to keep the specific *technical skills* of the job honed. You can also talk about how you used other *transferable skills* and applied *professional values* in whatever work you were doing, noting that these skills are fresh, current, and needed in every job.

What would your references say?

You have nothing to lose by giving a positive answer. If you checked your references, you can give details of what your best reference will say. When you demonstrate how well you and your boss got along, the interviewer does not have to ask, "What do you dislike about your current manager?"

Read the more extensive section on references in *Knock 'em Dead: The Ultimate Job Search Guide*, Chapter 3 and Chapter 19.

What aspects of your work do you consider most crucial?

Your answer begins with an explanation of why the job exists and what role it plays in achieving departmental and company goals.

Then itemize the most important responsibilities of the job (you prioritized these in your *TJD*).

You then proceed to address:

- The *technical skills* you need to deliver on these responsibilities: "I need to be able to do [*technical skills*] to execute my responsibilities."
- "Of course, crucial to the job is my ability to *identify, prevent, and solve* the problems that crop up in each of these areas every day. . . ."
- Selections of *transferable skills* that help you deliver on these crucial responsibilities: "So my *multitasking, communication,* and *critical thinking skills* help me do this every day. . . ."

How do you manage your work deadlines?

This examines the *time management* and *organization abilities* that enable you to *multitask* productively. You should address the Prioritize, Do, Review cycle: You set time at the end of every day to review that day's activities and plan tomorrow's. You prioritize all the planned activities and stick to those priorities to make sure the important work is attended to first.

> **What annoys you?** Someone who rambles and doesn't have a logical approach to answering questions.
>
> Al Daum, CPC. Alan N. Daum & Associates. Process automation engineering. 36 years' experience.

Describe to me how your job contributes to the overall goals of your department and company.

Every company is in business to make a profit. Every company depends on individual initiative being harnessed to *teamwork* to achieve the complex tasks that result in corporate profitability. Describe how your job makes individual contributions and its role as an important cog in the machinery that is your department. Your cog needs to mesh with all the other cogs (your colleagues) for the gears of productivity to engage and move the department toward its goals.

Show that you are aware of the problems that crop up in your job every day and get in the way of company productivity. Identify how your job, at its core, is to *anticipate and prevent problems* from arising and to *solve them* when they do.

What is your greatest strength?

First talk about a must-have *technical skill*. Second, talk about one or more of the *transferable skills* that help you execute this critical part of your job; for example, you could talk about the roles that *communication, critical thinking*, and *multitasking skills* play in helping you execute your "greatest strength." This way you give a complete and believable answer that also speaks to skills you apply in other aspects of your work.

What is your greatest weakness?

We all share a weakness: staying current with rapid changes in technology. The changes in technology give everyone an ongoing challenge: getting up to speed with the new skills demanded if you are to do your job well. Your answer can address this very issue, and in the process you will show yourself as someone capable of staying on top of things in a rapidly changing workplace.

First talk about these constantly evolving challenges, then follow with examples that show how you *are* keeping up with technologies that affect your productivity: "I'm currently reading about . . ."; "I just attended a weekend workshop . . ."; or "I'm signed up for classes at . . ."

With this type of answer you identify your weakness as something *that is only of concern to the most dedicated and forward-looking professionals in your field*.

You could also talk about the general difficulties in keeping up with all the deliverables of the job, and use it to talk about what you are doing to develop your *multitasking skills*. You can also consider the following as effective alternatives or as additional illustrations if they are demanded.

- If there is a *minor* part of the target job where you lack knowledge—but knowledge you will pick up quickly—use that.
- Give a generalized answer that takes advantage of *professional values*. Design the answer so that your weakness is ultimately a positive characteristic. For example: "I enjoy my work and always give my best. So when others are not pulling their weight, I find it annoying, and it is a real weakness. I am aware of this, and in those situations I try to overcome it with a positive attitude and just stick to doing my part well."

How do you go about solving problems in your work?

There is an established approach to problem solving that everyone who gets ahead in her professional life learns: When confronted with a problem, you take these steps:

- Define the problem.
- Identify why it's a problem and for whom it's a problem.
- Identify what's causing the problem.
- Seek input from everyone affected by the problem.
- Identify possible solutions.
- Identify the time, cost, and resources it will take to implement each option.
- Evaluate the consequences of each solution.
- Decide upon the best solution, based on these considerations.
- Identify and execute the steps necessary to solve the problem.

What is your role as a team member?

Think for a moment about why the job exists: It is there to contribute to the bottom line in some way. Your department, in turn, has a similar but larger role in the company's bottom line. Your ability to link your job's role to that of the department's larger responsibilities, and then to the overall success of the company, will demonstrate your sense of the importance of teamwork. The department depends on teamwork, so describe yourself as a *team player*.

What kinds of decisions are most difficult for you?

The most difficult decisions always relate to the most crucial responsibilities of your work. The employer is looking for people who can make decisions and solve problems, not those who'll dither instead of do. You want to position yourself as someone who's decisive but not precipitate, who considers the implications of decisions, any side effects they might have on other activities, and whether the decision conflicts with existing *systems and procedures* or other company priorities. Emphasize that, having analyzed the situation and reached a logical conclusion, you act.

The question almost demands that you explain how you make these difficult decisions, and that you give an illustration, and if you don't give one, it might well come in a follow-up question. Your example should relate to one of the crucial responsibilities of your job, and itemize the logical steps you take in analyzing the problem to help you reach the right decision.

> **Interviewer peeves.** That you have to look at your resume to remember things. Asking what our company does. Unprepared. No research.
>
> Nancy C. Anton, CPC. Talent Consultant, CIGNA. 20 years' experience.

What bothers you most about your job?

Keep your answer focused on those aspects of your work that *everyone* agrees are annoying, and end your answer on a positive note about how you deal with them: You take the rough with the smooth, and take the time to do [whatever it is that bothers you] well so you don't have to do the damn thing over. It is important that your answer show you remaining objective and calm.

Describe a situation where your work or an idea of yours was criticized.

This is a doubly dangerous question because you are being asked to describe how you handle criticism, and to detail inadequacies. If you have the choice, describe a poor idea that was criticized, not poor work.

Put your example in the past, make it small, and show what you learned from the experience. Show that you go through these steps to become maximally productive:

- Listen to understand.
- Confirm the understanding.
- Ask for guidance.
- Confirm the desired outcome.
- Show a satisfactory resolution.
- Address what you learned and how the experience helped you grow.

Your answer shows you are objective, that you listen for understanding and don't just wait your turn to talk. You confirm your understanding of what has been said and what is expected, and show that a satisfactory resolution was ultimately reached as a result of the input and how you implemented it. In closing, you recognize the positive impact of the manager, then demonstrate what you learned and how your thinking/approach has changed as a result.

Tell me about a time things went wrong.

You are asked to talk about something that went wrong, but that doesn't mean you can't do so with an example that turned out fine. Your *TJD* process identified a number of such examples you can use. Choose an example and paint it black, but don't point the finger of blame; crap happens.

End with how you solved, or contributed to the solution, of the problem. Get in a subtle plug for *professional values*: ". . . so sticking with it and doing it by the book helped us put things right in the end."

You can go on to explain that the next time you faced the same kind of problem you had a better frame of reference, knew what to avoid, what to do more of, and what other new approaches you could try. Finish your answer with a statement about what you learned.

How have you benefited from your disappointments/mistakes?

You learn more from failures, mistakes, and errors than you do from successes, so this is an opportunity for you to demonstrate your *emotional maturity* (you stay calm) and *critical thinking skills* (you think things through objectively).

Your answer will explain how you treat setbacks as learning experiences: you look at what happened, why it happened, and how you can do things differently at each stage. You don't need to be specific about your failures, but be prepared with an example in case of a follow-up question starting, "Tell me about a time when. . . ."

Failure Profile: The technophobe. If you are the person who continuously asks younger colleagues how to do things or won't learn new software, you will be targeted. One role/one job is fading fast, if not already gone.

Nancy Schuman, CSP. Corporate VP Marketing, Lloyd Staffing. 30 years' experience.

Have you ever had any financial difficulties?

Tell the truth because when references are checked, salary and credit are at the top of the list. However, do not bring up financial problems until this question is asked or an offer is on the table. Your answer succinctly gives the circumstances, the facts of your difficulties, and where you stand today in resolving these issues.

For someone to check your credit history, he must have your written consent. This is required under the 1972 Fair Credit and Reporting Act. Invariably, when you fill out a job application form, sign it, and date it, you've also signed a release permitting the employer to check your credit history.

If you have had to file for bankruptcy, it will show up in a credit check, so be honest, professional, and brief. Don't give any info about the circumstances: They aren't necessary and no one wants to know. What an employer does want to hear is that you have turned the corner and everything is under control now. They also want to know, very briefly, what you learned and have done to rebuild your credit. Financial difficulties aren't the deal-breaker they used to be, unless they affect the employer's insurance obligations. In light of the corporate and personal financial crises of recent years, many corporations are re-evaluating and taking a more realistic stance on these matters. Once it's behind you, get it expunged from your record.

How should I handle a DWI?

Find out if it will show up, as this differs from state to state. If the application asks, answer and leave it be; if not, don't offer this information until background checks are close. Then be brief—"It happened, I was young, etc."—and stress what you learned from it. Try to get it expunged: Google "DWI expunge."

How should I handle a felony?

First determine if it's on your record, if it will show up in a background check, and what employers in your state can take into consideration. States handle felony records differently from one another, as they do the information an employer may inquire about. Learn what you have to disclose to an employer and don't disclose more than you have to. Briefly, tell the employer what you've learned and that it is behind you. Discrepancies between your application and convictions can cause problems. There's no need to discuss issues that didn't result in conviction or anything that has been expunged.

As soon as you start asking questions, it becomes more of a conversation and less of an interview. Keep in mind that many interviewers can be nervous and awkward as well. Look for common ground with the interviewer, and be positive; every interview is a learning experience.

Rich Gold, CPC. Senior Recruiter, Smith Arnold Partners. Finance recruiter. 20 years' experience.

How do I get the best out of you? Or ***How did your boss get the best out of you?***

The interviewer could be envisioning you as an employee. Encourage the thought by describing a supportive manager who outlined projects and expected results at the start, noted deadlines, shared her greater experience and perspectives, and told you about potential problems. She always shared the benefit of experience. You agreed on a plan of attack for the work, and how and when you needed to give status updates along the way. Your boss was always available for advice, preferred giving it early or late in the day, and taught you to take the work seriously but encouraged a collegial team atmosphere.

What are you looking for in your next job?

Ask not what your company can do for you, ask what you can do for your company. You are there to get a job offer, and only want to address your needs when an offer is on the table and negotiation likely.

With so little real knowledge about the company—your research isn't the same as insights explained by a company representative—you need to be careful about specificity.

Keep your answer general, and focus your answer on the fulfillment you experience from a job well done, with a team similarly committed, working for a company with a solid reputation. If you're lower on the success ladder, add learned and earned professional growth to this; if your future boss is the next step up . . . not such a good idea.

What do you spend most of your time on, and why?

Your answer obviously needs to show that you focus your attention on top priorities, and you can make additional points by noting that you don't ignore the repetitive tasks that are also important and sometimes require considerable time. You mention some small thing that has to be done frequently, because if it has to be done frequently, it is obviously critical to success.

Another tactic is to use an example of *multitasking* to emphasize how you manage the priorities of the job. For example, "Like a lot of businesspeople, I work on the telephone and meetings take up a great deal of time. What's important to me is prioritization of activities based on the deliverables of my job. I find more gets achieved in a shorter time if a meeting is scheduled, say, immediately before lunch or at the close of business. I try to block my time in the morning and the afternoon for main thrust activities. At four o'clock, I review what I've achieved, what went right or wrong, and plan adjustments and my main thrust for tomorrow."

What are your qualifications for this job?

The interviewer is interested in your experience and your possession of the *technical skills* to do the job, your academic qualifications, and the *transferable skills* that enable you to do any task well; this is why you need a clear recall of which *transferable skills* help you execute which aspect of your job. If you are confident in your skills, you can learn more about the job, and make points for your candidacy, by asking a question of your own: "If you could tell me about specific work assignments I'll be involved with early on, I can show exactly how I can make real contributions in this job."

What can you do for us that someone else cannot do?

You cannot know other candidates' capabilities, so smilingly disarm your interviewer with this fact, then say, "But what I bring is. . . ." Your answer will then demonstrate your grasp of the job's responsibilities, the problems that occur in each area, and how you are prepared to deal with them.

You can finish your answer with reference to the *transferable skills* and *professional values* you also bring to the job: "I also bring to this job a *determination* to see projects through to a proper conclusion. I *listen* and take direction well. I am *analytical* and don't jump to conclusions. I understand we are in business to make a *profit*, so I keep an eye on cost and return." End with: "How do these qualifications fit your needs?" or "What else are you looking for?" If you haven't covered the interviewer's hot buttons, he will cover them now, and you can respond accordingly.

Nervous? There's nothing wrong with saying, "I'm nervous because I really want to come work for your organization." Flattery will buy you some time but don't rely upon it solely.

Karen McGrath, PHR. Talent Acquisition Manager, Enterprise Rent-A-Car.
22 years' experience.

How do you stay current?

We live in an age of technological innovation, in which the nature of every job is changing as quickly as you turn these pages. This means you must look to professional education as the price of sustained employability. In your answer, talk about the importance of keeping abreast of changes in the profession. You can refer to:

- Courses you have taken or are planning to take
- Books you have read or are reading
- Membership in professional associations or online groups
- Subscriptions to professional journals

What achievements are you most proud of?

Use an example of something you did as an individual or some larger project, where you were part of a team. Don't exaggerate your contributions to major projects—share the success and be seen as a *team player*. Be honest, and to guarantee your illustrations are relevant, take them from your *TJD*. For example, you might say something like, "Although I feel my biggest achievements are still ahead of me, I am proud of my involvement with _____. I made my contribution as part of that team and learned a lot in the process."

Tell me about the most difficult project you've tackled.

When possible, discuss projects that parallel work you are likely to do at the new job. You will state the project, its challenges in some detail, your *critical thinking* process to isolate causes and possible solutions, the story of your implementation of the solution, and the value it delivered to your employer.

What do you think of your current/last boss? How could she have done a better job?

Never criticize management. No manager is going to hire someone likely to affect productivity and make her job more difficult. Be short, sweet, and shut up. You liked and respected that manager, and appreciated her guidance and encouragement to grow.

What have you learned from jobs you have held?

You've learned that little gets achieved without *teamwork* and that there's invariably sound thinking behind *systems and procedures*. To get to the root of problems it's better to talk less and listen more. Most of all, you've learned that you can either sit on the sidelines watching the hours go by or you can get involved and make a difference with your presence. You do the latter because you're goal-oriented, time goes quicker when you're engaged, and besides, the relationships you build are with better people.

Tell me about an important goal you set recently.

Your answer should cite a goal that relates to productivity or another aspect related to the more important deliverables of your job in some way. You might use a skill-development goal, explaining why you chose it, how it helped you grow, and the benefits of completion. Or you can talk about a productivity/performance standard goal, why you chose it, and how it helped. You can add to this how you integrated achieving this goal into all your other activities, which allows you to talk about your *multitasking skills*.

> **There are people who don't realize** that they don't have good *critical thinking skills.* They have been taught to accept what is told them and have never developed the ability to look at a situation and come up with their own solutions.
>
> Marjean Bean, CPC. President, Medit Staff. Information technology. 30+ years' experience.

What have you done to become more effective in your job?

Similarly to the prior question, behind this is an interest in your motivation to do the work being offered. The interviewer is looking for a fit between your dreams and his reality. All worthwhile jobs require hard work and a desire to learn.

Technology changes mean your job skills must always be in development if you want to remain current and viable. The interviewer wants to know if you are *committed* to your profession and is looking for *at least* one example. You can also talk of the mentor relationships you have formed, the books and professional commentary you've read, the professional organizations you belong to, the certifications you're earning, courses you are enrolled in, and webinars you attend. If you aren't doing some of these things, wake up and start NOW.

What do you do when there is a decision to be made and no procedure exists?

You need to show that even though you're more than capable of taking initiative, you're not a rogue missile. Explain that the first thing you'll do will be to discuss the situation with your boss or—if time is tight and this isn't possible—with peers. That's exactly what the hiring manager wants to hear. Make clear that in developing any new approach/procedure/idea you'll stick to the company's established *systems and procedures*.

How do you rank among your peers?

The interviewer is examining your self-esteem. In some cases (for instance in sales) it may be possible for you to quantify this: "I'm number two in the region." In other cases, you'll be more subjective, but you should strive to be realistic. You might slip in a real-life detail such as, "There are two groups in my department: those who make a difference, and those who watch. I'm in the first group."

How do you feel about your progress to date?

Your answer should illustrate a commitment to productivity and illustrate the effort you invest in professional development. Explain how you ensure that your work is executed effectively and, if you can, cite endorsements given you by managers. You see each day as an opportunity to learn and contribute, and you see the environment at this company as conducive to your best efforts. Perhaps say something like, "Given the parameters of my job, my progress has been excellent. I know the work, and I am just reaching that point in my career where I can make significant contributions."

You might finish by saying that being at this interview means you've gone as far as you can with your present employer and that this environment at _____ and its new ways will encourage a new spurt of growth.

Is it ever necessary to go above and beyond the call of duty in terms of effort or time to get your job done?

On the one hand corporate culture encourages burning the midnight oil, yet many managers are leery of people who portray themselves as coming into the office at 3:00 A.M. on Sunday to get the job done. Your answer is most effective when you say, "Yes" and then illustrate with a story of making extra and special efforts.

Impress—ability to communicate and connect to people.
Annoy—evasive answers and lack of candor.

Jim Rohan, Senior Partner, J P Canon Associates. Supply chain management. 25 years' experience.

Tell me about a time when an emergency caused you to reschedule your workload/projects.

The question examines how you handle emergency imperatives. You'll make points when you add that your strong *planning and time management skills* not only see you through high-pressure situations, they also allow you to stay on top of your regular responsibilities.

The story you tell should illustrate your flexibility and willingness to work extra hours when necessary. Demonstrate that your *multitasking skills* allow you to change course without having a nervous breakdown.

How long will it take you to make a contribution?

It takes time to understand *systems and procedures*, who the power players are, and why things are done the way they are. Be sure to qualify the question: In what area does the interviewer need rapid contributions?

You might ask, "Where are your greatest areas of need right now?" You give yourself time to think while the interviewer explains priorities.

How do you take direction?

This question translates as: Can you follow directions and accept constructive criticism, or are you a difficult, high-maintenance employee? In this context we can define manageability as your willingness to take direction and criticism when it is carefully and considerately given, and the ability also to accept criticism when it isn't carefully and considerately given, perhaps because of a crisis.

Make it clear that you can take constructive criticism because that is how you learn and improve, and that your first priority is to get the job done in the best way possible.

If you could make one constructive suggestion to management, what would it be?

What matters here is less the specific content of your answer than the tone. Suggest what you know to be true and what your interviewer will appreciate as a breath of fresh air: Most people want to do a good job. Management should create an environment where striving for excellence is encouraged *and* where those retired on the job have the opportunity to change their ways or leave. Everyone would benefit.

What is the most difficult situation you have faced?

You're really being asked two different questions: "What do you consider difficult?" and "How did you handle it?" This means the interviewer will be evaluating both your *critical thinking* and *technical skills*.

Don't talk about problems with coworkers in your answer. Instead, focus on a job-related problem. We have talked about the importance of problem solving throughout the book, and the steps a professional takes to identify the most appropriate approaches and solutions; you should have numerous examples from your *TJD* and the resume creation process with which to illustrate your answer. In ending your answer, be sure to identify the benefits of your solution.

> **Success profile.** More emphasis is placed on attitude as companies appreciate they not only need knowledge and skills, they need flexible people who can reinvent themselves with new knowledge, skills, and abilities as opportunities and challenges arise.
>
> Dr. Jim Bright, Partner, Bright & Associates, Australia. Author, *Chaos Theory of Careers*. 22 years' experience.

What have you done that shows initiative?

The story you tell shows you stepping up to do a job others didn't see or didn't want to do, but which nevertheless needed to be done. For example, "Every quarter, I sit down with my boss and find out the dates of all her meetings for the next six months. I immediately make the hotel and flight arrangements, and attend to all the web-hosting details. I ask myself questions like, 'If the agenda for the July meeting is to reach the field at least six weeks before the meeting, when must it be finished by?' Then I come up with a deadline. I do that for all the major activities for all the meetings. I put the deadlines in her PDA, and in mine two weeks earlier to ensure everything is done on time. My boss is the best-organized, most relaxed manager in the company."

Why do you feel you are a better manager/assistant than some of your coworkers?

The trick is to answer the question without showing yourself in anything but a flattering light. "I don't spend my time thinking about how I am better than my colleagues, because that would be detrimental to our working together as a team. I believe, however, some of the qualities that make me an outstanding _____ are. . . ." From here, go on to itemize specific *technical skills* of your profession where you are particularly strong, and a couple of the *transferable skills* that apply to doing these aspects of your work so well.

> **Success profile.** On the job, you play well for the team and share credit, while making your own contributions clear. You look out for yourself, but help others wherever you can, thereby building long-term relationships.
>
> Marsha Connolly, Managing Partner, The New River Group. Certified Executive Coach. 30 years' experience.

Have you ever had to make unpopular decisions?

Inherent in the question is a request for an example, in which you'll demonstrate how *critical thinking* and *leadership skills* help you make the unpopular decision, while *teamwork* and *communication skills* help make it palatable. Your answer needs to show that you're not afraid to make unpopular decisions when they are in the best interests of your job or the department's goals.

Simultaneously, stress your effort to make the decision workable for all parties and finish by explaining how everyone subsequently accepted its necessity and got on board.

In working with new people, how do you go about getting an understanding of them?

Every new hire is expected to become a viable part of the group, which means getting an understanding of the group and its individual members. Understanding that everyone likes to give advice is the key to your answer. You have found that the best way to understand and become part of a new team is to be open, friendly, ask lots of questions, and be helpful whenever you can. The answers to your questions give you needed insights into the ways of the job, department, and company, and they help you get to know the person.

Define "cooperation."

The question examines *manageability* and asks you to explain how you see your responsibilities as a *team player*, both taking direction and working for the overall success of your department. Your answer will include an explanation of "cooperation" as doing your job in a way that enables your colleagues to do theirs with a minimum of disruption. It's your desire by hard work and goodwill to be part of something significant: making the team something greater than the sum of its parts.

What do you think determines progress in a good company?

The interviewer needs to see that you understand progress is earned over time, and does not come as a result of simply showing up to work on a regular basis. Begin with each of the *technical skills* required to do the job, briefly citing the *transferable skill* that allows you to do the job well. Finish with your *willingness* to take the rough with the smooth that goes with every job, and the good fortune of having a manager who wants you to succeed.

What are some of the problems you encounter in doing your job, and what do you do about them?

Refer to your *TJD* for all the information you'll need to identify responsibilities, employer priorities, and the problems that occur in these areas and how you handle them. Then you'll be able to give an example in an area you know is critical to the interviewer.

You might add at the end, "Some aspects of my job are fairly repetitive, so it's easy to skip things, but that causes problems down the line."

If I hired you today, what would you accomplish first?

Gear your answer to first getting settled in the job, understanding how things are done, and becoming a member of the team. You will mention that of course this includes the clear priority of all your responsibilities. Then finish with a question, "What are the most critical projects/problems you'll want me to tackle?" The response to that becomes your final answer to what you will accomplish first.

What type of decisions do you make in your work?
This examines the extent of your authority and how *critical thinking* enters into your work. With the *TJD*, you will have a clear understanding of the job's deliverables and can determine the decision-making events that are integral to your job. The interviewer will certainly follow with a request for an example. Assume this will happen and your answer will address the types of decisions you make, and include an example that shows how you approach making them.

> **Interviewer peeves.** Answers are often too vague, so there's a ton of follow-up questions. Answer the questions more fully and you'll be more satisfied with the flow of the interview.
> Karen McGrath, PHR. Talent Acquisition Manager, Enterprise Rent-A-Car. 22 years' experience.

How do you handle rejection?
The interviewer wants to know whether you take rejection personally or simply accept it as a temporary rejection of a service or product.

Here is a sample answer for people in sales that you can tailor to your particular needs no matter what your job: "I accept rejection as an integral part of the sales process. If everyone said 'yes' to a product, there would be no need for the sales function. As it is, I see every rejection as bringing me closer to the customer who will say 'yes.' Sales is a profession of *communication, determination,* and *resiliency*; rejection is just part of the process. I always try to leave the potential customer with a good feeling, as no sale today can become a sale next month."

Tell me about a situation that frustrated you at work.
This question is about *emotional maturity*. The interviewer wants to know how you channel frustration into productivity. Give an example of a difficult situation in which you remained diplomatic, objective, and found a solution that benefited all concerned. Show yourself to be someone who isn't managed by *emotions*: You acknowledge the

frustration, then put it aside in favor of achieving the goals of the job you are paid to do.

What interests you least about this job?

The question is potentially explosive but easily defused. Regardless of your occupation, there is at least one repetitive, mindless duty that everyone groans about, but which nevertheless goes with the territory. Use that as your example. "_____ are probably the least demanding part of my job. However, I know they are important for _____, so I do them at the end of the day as part of my performance review and next day planning." Notice how this response also shows that you are *organized,* and possess *critical thinking* and *multitasking skills.*

> **How to fail.** Focus on "what's in it for me?"—put [management] in a position where every simple job-related task or request becomes a negotiation. Be intolerant of the short-term sacrifices that lead to the greatest long-term rewards.
>
> Rick Kean, Consultant Emeritus, A. M. Hamilton, Inc. Staffing and training. 30+ years' experience.

Tell me a story.

What on earth does the interviewer mean by that question? It is asked, in part, to see how analytical you are: People who answer the question without qualifying show they do not think things through carefully. It can also be asked, in part again, to get a glimpse of the things you hold important.

Ask, "What would you like me to tell you a story about?" The answer you get to your question may give you direction, or it may not; but either way it demonstrates your *critical thinking* skills.

I'm not sure you're suitable for the job (too inexperienced).

In a job search you quickly develop a feeling for whether a particular position is a close match, a job you've already done for so long that you might be perceived as too experienced (too heavy), or a job that might be a bit of a stretch (too light). If you can see a potential problem with an opportunity, the employer probably can too. Nevertheless, you were close enough to get the interview, so make every effort to land the offer.

When you might be too light, your answer itemizes all the experience and skills you bring, and offsets weaknesses with other strengths and examples of how efficiently you develop new skills. You can also talk about the motivation you bring to the job, and that you will expect to be motivated for some time while someone with all the skills is going to be after a promotion to keep her happy.

I'm not sure you're suitable for the job (too experienced).

If you are told you have too much experience, respond with the positives: how your skills help you deliver immediately, and why the position fits your needs. Perhaps say, "I really enjoy my work, so I won't get bored, and I'm not looking for a promotion, so I'm not after anyone's job. I'll be a reliable and trustworthy person to have at your back. I have excellent skills [itemize], so I can deliver quickly and consistently. My experience makes me a steadying member of the team and when you think I'm ready I can help mentor." Finish with a smile, ". . . and let's not forget I've already made my mistakes on somebody else's payroll."

Do you have any questions?

A sign that the interview is drawing to a close. Take the opportunity to make a strong impression. Ask questions that help advance your candidacy, by giving you information about the real-world experience of the job: "Yes I do have one or two questions." Go through the list of questions you developed after reading the interview preparation chapter and brought with you.

- Who succeeds in this job and why?
- Who fails in this job and why?
- What are the major projects of the first six months?
- What will my first assignment be?

Most candidates ask questions about money and benefits. These are nice-to-know questions that an interviewer is not really interested in discussing at this point. As your goal at every interview is to bring the interviewer to the point of offering you the job, such questions are really irrelevant because they don't bring you closer to the job offer. Better that you concentrate on gathering information that will help you further your candidacy.

Ask about next steps—if there are more interviews. If there are, match your skills to the needs of the job, explain your interest in the job and desire to pursue it: Ask for the next interview.

If there's not another interview, cite your understanding of the job, how your skills match each of the deliverables, that you want the job, want to join the team, and ask for the job.

The success headset. After interviewing with both a commercial construction firm and a property management firm, an architectural assistant ended up with both offers. The reason: She did her homework, researched both companies, wrote personal thank-you notes for the positions, had excellent references, and was completely reasonable on the compensation issues.

Glenna Cose Brin, CPC. President, AllianceStaff. High-end administration. 30+ years' experience.

Resources

- For further discussion of tactics for turning interviews into job offers, see the entire second half of *Knock 'em Dead: The Ultimate Job Search Guide*, latest annual edition.
- For job search letter templates for interview follow-up, resurrection, negotiation, acceptance, rejection, and resignation letters, visit *www.knockemdead.com*.

CHAPTER 12

OUT OF SIGHT CAN MEAN OUT OF MIND

Studies have shown that the last person interviewed more frequently gets the job, but this isn't always the case by any means. Even if you are the last one interviewed, the longer the decision-making period, the less distinct candidates become from each other in the hiring manager's memory. You leave your interviewers with a strong, positive image, and you don't want that memory to slip with the passage of time and a busy schedule. We've noted that in tightly run job races the offer invariably goes to the candidate who is most *intelligently enthusiastic*; following up on your interviews demonstrates this and is noted both in the breach and the observance. The written word stays in memory longer and with greater clarity than conversations, because it can be reread. A good follow-up strategy could well be the deciding factor in who gets the job offer if the race is tight between you and another candidate.

Most companies prefer to hire someone who wants to work there. Follow-up shows you are interested and lets the interviewer know you want the job.

Marjean Bean, CPC. President, Medit Staff. Information technology.
30+ years' experience.

As soon as you can after the interview, make notes on what happened. The information will help with your follow-up with this company, and reviewing all your follow-up notes after two or three interviews may alert you to a weakness you hadn't noticed. *Self-awareness, that rare ability to look at oneself objectively, is always the first step in fixing behavioral and performance problems.* Make notes on these categories:

- Who did you meet? What were their titles and e-mail addresses?
- What did you find out about the job?
- What are its first projects/challenges?
- Why can you do it? What are the problems?
- What went right and why?
- What went less well?
- What did the interviewer say on any topic related to the job, company, competition, industry, or profession that might give you a unique follow-up, were you to Google something interesting?
- What was a royal screw-up and why?
- What did the interviewer say was the next step?
- Are there other candidates in contention?
- When will a decision be made?
- What did the interviewer say in concluding the interview?

Using the information gathered from this exercise, you can begin a follow-up campaign. Knowing if there is another round of interviews or if the decision is going to be made tomorrow afternoon or next week has significant impact on how and when you will follow up.

Definitely noticed if a candidate does not send a thank-you note. More than just common courtesy, these managers are looking for the candidate's follow-up and communication skills.

Denise Wilkerson, RN, CPC. Executive Search Director, Global Edge Recruiting. Medical devices, biotech, pharma, sales/marketing management. 14+ years' experience.

The majority of my colleagues suggest you follow up within twenty-four hours, and I agree *if this is the final interview and the decision is imminent*; but when the decision is not imminent (the next seventy-two hours)—when there are more interviews in the cycle and/or the decision is further away—I think a differently paced schedule is required. In these circumstances the formal follow-up letter's job is to re-energize and maintain visibility of your candidacy when memory of it is beginning to slip with the passage of time and is blurred by other candidates.

Follow-Up Steps and Pacing

Knowing where you are in the selection cycle will help you execute a well-paced follow-up campaign. We'll start with follow-up after the first interview in a series.

After the First Interview in a Series

1. INFORMAL FIRST FOLLOW-UP WITHIN TWENTY-FOUR HOURS

> **Don't say** you understand I need to see more people, it makes you sound unsure of yourself.
>
> Karen McGrath, PHR. Talent Acquisition Manager, Enterprise Rent-A-Car. 22 years' experience.

If you can find something interesting related to the job, company, competition, industry, or profession, your first follow-up will be professional-casual, reinforcing the tone of an ongoing conversation between two professionals with a common interest. You'll send an e-mail that opens with a salutation: "Hi John/Jane," if you are close enough in years and experience to use first names. If you are younger and have been encouraged to use first names, it's okay too, but reverting to the formalities of "Mr./Ms." in written communication (until after the second meeting), will usually be received as respectful and flattering. If use of first names hasn't been encouraged, don't presume: It won't win you points, while showing professional courtesies always does.

This informal follow-up e-mail has a short, casual, two-professionals-talking tone that is only appropriate if rapport was established:

"It was great to meet you this afternoon. I really enjoyed talking about the _____ position. Your comments/our conversation on _____ [the topic of your attachment, or what you paste into the body copy] has been buzzing in the back of my mind all day. I just ran across this and knew you'd enjoy it. On a deadline, so I'll follow up properly as soon as my schedule permits."

Send the e-mail between 7:00 P.M. and 10:00 P.M. that evening or early the next morning when you first get up, whichever is closer to the twenty-four-hour mark. Do not send an e-mail during business hours.

Your first meeting will have tagged you as someone different. This initial follow-up aims to continue the differentiation. The tone is respectful, shows a committed professional working late (you can't write fully because you are working on a deadline), and *intelligently enthusiastic* (you are actively engaged in thinking about this job and your profession outside of business hours).

2. FORMAL FIRST FOLLOW-UP

Your formal first follow-up should arrive two to no later than three days after the first interview, OR after your first *informal* follow-up, adjusting your timing to the needs of each separate selection cycle. This formal follow-up letter should make the following points:

- The date and time you met with the interviewer and the title of the target job
- You paid attention to what was said in the interview
- Why you can do the job
- You are excited about the job and want it
- You have the experience to contribute to those first major projects as discussed in the interview

Adding New Information

Your follow-up note is also a good opportunity to add new information that you realize would be relevant, to answer any questions you didn't adequately address, or to introduce any aspects of your experience that you forgot in the heat of the moment. You can say something along the lines of, "On reflection, I . . ." or "Having thought about our meeting, I thought I'd mention . . ." or "I should have mentioned that . . ."

Keep the note short (less than one page) and address it to the hiring manager or main interviewer if you haven't met your new boss yet. If you interviewed with other people and the meeting was more than cursory, you can send separate e-mails to each.

> **If something went wrong** (the company wanted someone with international business experience and you don't have that), address that point: "While I do not have business experience abroad, I have traveled extensively throughout Europe and do speak German."
>
> Alesia Benedict, CPRW, JCTC. CEO, GetInterviews.com. Resumes, social media. 20+ years' experience.

Additional Interviews

If the selection cycle is normal, three interviews for each of a handful of short-list candidates can take three or four weeks, so with the second and subsequent interviews (excepting the final interview), your follow-up pattern should replicate that of the initial interview.

1. An informal follow-up within twenty-four hours, essentially saying:

> "Good to see you again Jack, and to meet the guys.
> Thanks for your time. Preparing for a client meeting;
> I'll get back to you properly in the next couple of days."

You might replace this with an equally brief phone call, when there is something to warrant a brief conversation. If the manager doesn't pick up, leave a complete but brief message. You don't need to call back.

2. A formal follow-up, following the same principles and timing as before. As the interview cycle progresses, you want to maintain awareness of your candidacy, but you don't want to be seen as doing anything by rote.

Although the bulk of business correspondence these days is done via e-mail, remember that a traditional letter can make you stand out.

> **Follow-up should be strategic,** not stalker-like. Each follow-up should add something, perhaps to cover things that went unaddressed in the interview.
>
> Jim Rohan, Senior Partner, J P Canon Associates. Supply chain management. 25 years' experience.

Additional Interviews and Extended Interview Cycles

You don't want to make a pest of yourself by calling or e-mailing every day, but neither do you want to drop out of sight. If the process stretches out into a month or months, make contact every couple of weeks, but keep it very low-volume. You don't want to seem overly anxious, just interested.

As you did before, you might send profession-relevant information:

"Harry, being so busy you may not have seen the article I've attached. It's about new legislation that's bound to affect us.

Regards,
Martin

P.S. I'm still determined to be your next _____."

You can do this in an e-mail and/or by traditional mail. Getting a funny e-mail always brightens the day, and giving the interviewer a smile is a great way to be remembered, but this requires judgment. Don't send anything of a sexual, political, or religious nature, as it constitutes a breach of *professional values*.

The same considerations apply when sending a cartoon via traditional mail. This works because it's a different delivery medium and the cartoon causes a smile; plus, if you're lucky, the cartoon gets stuck on the wall or passed on.

Can you be too aggressive? Yes; if I sense desperation, especially if I have set a candidate's expectation on timing, and keep them apprised of their candidacy, then I get annoyed, and wonder if this is how the candidate will act on the job.

Bob Waldo, Principal Consultant, Best Hire Consulting Services. 20+ years' experience.

Reposted Jobs

Sometimes jobs remain open for a long time, or they may be frozen because of budgetary constraints and reposted under a different job title. In these instances, go through an attenuated *TJD* exercise with the new job title to make sure the job hasn't changed in any meaningful ways, and that you have all the relevant keywords. If you're still in touch with the hiring manager or recruiter, send her the customized and updated version of your resume, noting the changes in her needs, and make a subsequent follow-up call.

The longer the hiring process drags on, the less likely it is that you will get the offer. It can happen, but the odds get longer as time goes by. Don't let your job search stand still while you're waiting for a response from one company. Remember: *You don't have the job until you have a written offer in hand.*

When the Hiring Decision Is Imminent

A decision next Friday means that an offer will be extended on that date, while the actual decision will be made *at least* seventy-two hours to five days prior, allowing HR the time to shepherd the paperwork through the authorization process. Of course, this isn't the case if you are interviewing for a job today and you are told that the decision will be made at the end of the week; as always, adapt your follow-up strategy to reflect the demands of the hiring cycle.

If you know in advance that a decision is coming, say Friday of the following week, you can aim to get an e-mail to the hiring manager this Friday/Monday; a slight variation of that message might arrive via traditional mail on the same or following day; and you can make a telephone call no later than Wednesday morning. This leaves seventy-two hours before decision time.

Final Written Communications
The content of these communications should cover:

- "We last met on _____ and have been talking about _____ job."
- "I can do the job and this is why: [talk about the *technical skills* you bring]."
- "I am excited about the job and this is why: [talk about how you can contribute to first projects and your desire to join a great group of people]."
- "I will make a good hire and this is why: [talk about the *transferable skills* and *professional values* you bring to the job]."
- "I want the job. What do I have to do to get it?"

Making That Final Call
If a hiring decision is imminent, succinctly following up on your e-mails and letters within seventy-two hours of decision time might help seal the deal. Work out what you want to say, write it down in bullet points, and make practice calls to friend, keeping it brief and to

the point. Then, when you are ready make the call, you have nothing to lose and a job offer to gain.

> **Job offers aren't always accepted.** Candidates who follow up land jobs they were not even competitive for, simply because they kept their names in front of the decision-maker. It happens more often than you imagine.
>
> Grant Cooper, President, Careerpro of New Orleans. Strategic Resumes. 17 years' experience.

Resources

For follow-up letter templates, visit *www.knockemdead.com*.

CHAPTER 13

JOB OFFER NEGOTIATIONS

A job offer will eventually be put on the table, probably after one or two approach questions:

Why should I hire you?
Keep your answer short and to the point. Demonstrate your grasp of the job's responsibilities, the problems typically occurring in each area, the *transferable skills* that allow you to consistently deliver on them, and then a brief review of what you are like as a professional colleague, personalizing the behavioral profile for success you identified in *TJD*. When you are a real contender this is a very common question. You need to prepare an answer before every new job interview; it prepares you for this question and, just as importantly, gets you hyper-focused on the requirements of each position.

What are you earning currently? Or *What were you making on your last job?*
Ideally the offer you negotiate should be based on salary norms and on the value you bring to the job. However, all too often an employer will want to base any forthcoming offer on your current salary.

If you are currently well-remunerated and just want a nice bump with your job change, this isn't a problem, but if you are underpaid it's a different situation. You might consider saying, "I am earning $XX,000, but I want you to know that a major reason for making a job change right now is to significantly increase my salary. I am currently underpaid for my skills, experience, and contributions, and my capabilities are under-utilized."

Education and salary are factors that very often get checked, and untruths in either of these areas are grounds for termination with cause.

The interviewer could ask to see a payroll stub or W2 form at the time you start work, or could make the offer dependent on verification of salary. A new employer may request verbal or written confirmation from previous employers or might use an outside verification agency.

In any instance where an employer checks references, credit, or other matters of verification, she is obliged by law to get your written permission. The impossibly small print on the bottom of the job application form—followed by a request for your signature—usually authorizes the employer to do just that.

How much money do you want?

If the question comes before you have enough details about the job, you can ask for more information: "I still have a few questions about my responsibilities, and it will be easier to talk about money when I've cleared them up. Could you explain. . . ."

When you have enough information, there is still a quandary: Ask for too much and you might not get an offer; ask for too little and you could be kicking yourself for years. The answer is to *come up with a salary range that puts you in the running, but doesn't nail you down to one specific dollar figure* that you might regret. All jobs have salary ranges attached to them. Your approach is to come up with a salary range for yourself. To help you get a general idea of what people are generally paid for this work:

- Try a salary calculator like *www.salary.com*.
- Compare ranges from job postings.
- Headhunters with whom you have a relationship may be able to help you with the salary range for your position within your target area.

You need to come up with a salary range specific to your circumstances. You do this in three steps:

1. Given your skills, experience, and location, determine the least you would accept for a suitable job with a stable company.
2. Given the same considerations, what would constitute a fair offer for a suitable job with a stable company.
3. Given the same considerations of skills, experience, and location, come up with the figure that would make you smile, drop dead, and go to heaven on the spot.

You will now have three figures: a minimum, a midpoint, and a dream salary. Kick out the lowest because you can always negotiate downward. This leaves you with a salary range—your midpoint to your high point—that you can give with confidence.

They Want You!

They want you but they don't have you. This is the first time you really have decisions to make: Do you want this job, and on what terms? The issues for your consideration are the job and its potential, the company and its stability, the money and the benefits. This is probably the only time in your relationship with your new employer when you'll have even a slim negotiating edge. If you under-negotiate your salary, that has an impact, not only today, but on your future earnings, because all raises will be based on a lower salary. Armed with this information, you can move the conversation forward.

> **Negotiation.** When you get an offer, the company wants you in that role, so you now have some room to negotiate.
>
> George Olmstead, Managing Partner, Olmstead Lynch & Kreutz. Senior management recruitment. 30 years' experience.

Step One

Open with, "If I understand the job correctly . . ." and then restate the responsibilities of the job as you understand them, building into your explanation what you know about the role of the job within the department, any initial or special projects, and any special needs that have come to light in your conversations. Your goal is to demonstrate your thorough grasp of the job. You want the interviewer muttering, "Wow, she really gets it!" Your dialogue sounds something like this: "If I'm qualified for this job, which I am because of A, B, C, D . . . I feel sure you'll make me a fair offer. What is the salary range for this position?"

You can be given a range, and if any part of that range intersects with *your* range, you reply, "Excellent! We certainly have something to talk about because I was looking for between $*XX,000* and $*YYY,000*. Obviously I'd like $*YYY,000*. How close do you think we can get?" or "That's certainly something we can talk about. I'm looking for between $*XX,000* with a maximum of $*YYY,000*. How much flexibility is there?"

Step Two

The interviewer can decline your request and ask again what you want. You reply with your salary range, which maximizes the chances of finding a match and minimizes the odds of asking for too much or too little.

> **Offers to entry level candidates** are rarely—if ever flexible. If you feel that the offer is good—don't feel compelled to ask for more . . . just because you don't want to accept a first offer.
>
> Sean Koppelman, President, The Talent Magnet. Advertising, beauty, and entertainment. 16 years' experience.

Once an Offer Is on the Table

Salaries are fairly standardized, so the majority of offers will come within your negotiating range. But even if the offer is fair or even exceptional, you can still negotiate.

The state of the job market can impact negotiations too: When supply exceeds demand negotiating upwards is harder. Nevertheless, with an offer on the table, the hiring manager has made the decision that he can hire you and get back to work; he and everyone else wants to be done with this project; negotiate in good faith and your negotiations will be accepted in the same way.

Biggest negotiation mistake? Realize that they may be low-balling by about 5–10 percent but that they really won't go much higher than that. If they're significantly below what you've made previously for the same duties and/or the industry average and an additional 10 percent won't get you where you need to be, walk away from the deal gracefully.

Michelle Hagans, Recruiter, Anu Resources Unlimited. IT and medical. 20+ years' experience.

Depending on where the offer is on your predetermined range, you can suggest that their offer is close to your low end and ask, "Is there any room for flexibility here?" You may get a bump since the first figure put on the table often isn't the best that can be offered; the worst that will happen is that the hiring manager will stick to the original offer.

Whatever the initial offer comes in at, always give it one realistic push for more. Then lower the tension by moving away from money and addressing other aspects of the package.

Always negotiate in a friendly, cooperative manner. Indicate your understanding of the restrictions the company is under and your appreciation for any flexibility they can show you. If the offer is really too low, the job may not be the right level job for you and it may be best to walk away. Never turn down the offer unless you are prepared to walk away.

Marsha Connolly, Managing Partner, The New River Group. Certified Executive Coach. 30 years' experience.

Questions to Evaluate the Job

Money is important, but your career trajectory moreso. New jobs are pivotal points in your life that affect not just this job and the next couple of years, but your whole life going forward. They shouldn't represent decisions made without thought or based purely on salary.

> **Often forgotten in the negotiation** are questions to evaluate if you want the job. "When will you measure my performance?" "What exactly will you be measuring?" The answers to questions like these are important.
>
> Bob Morris. Owner, Storage Placements. Data storage sales/marketing. 44 years' experience.

If you have plans for your life, this a step along your chosen path, so you want to land in an outfit that will help move you toward your goals. To find out, ask a few questions relevant to your situation:

The Job and Its Potential

- How long has the job been open?
- Why is it open? Who held the job last?
- What is he doing now? Promoted, fired, or quit?
- How long was he in that job?
- How many people have held this job in the last three years? Where are they now?
- How often have people been promoted from this position—and how many, and where to?
- Who in the company was in this position the shortest length of time? Why? Who has remained in this position the longest? Why?

Other questions that might follow include:

- What does it take to succeed in this job?
- Who fails in this job and why?

- What personality traits do you consider critical to success in this job?
- What kind of training does the company provide/encourage/support?
- How long have you held this position?
- Why did you choose to work here?
- Tell me about your management style.
- How often will we meet?
- How frequent are performance and salary reviews? Weighted toward merit and performance and if so how?
- How does the performance appraisal and reward system work? Exactly how are outstanding employees recognized, judged, and rewarded?
- To what extent are the functions of the department recognized as important and worthy of review by upper management?
- Where and how does my department fit into the foodchain?
- What does the department hope to achieve in the next two to three years? How will that help the company?
- What do you see as the strengths of the department? What do you see as weaknesses?
- What role do you hope I will play in the department?
- What informal and formal benchmarks will you use to measure my effectiveness and contributions?
- Based on my effectiveness, how long would you anticipate me holding this position?
- When my position and responsibilities change, what are the possible titles and responsibilities I might grow into?
- What is the official corporate policy on internal promotion? How many people in this department have been promoted from their original positions since joining the company?
- How do I pursue promotion and how do you determine my suitability?
- What training and professional development programs are available?
- How does the company support independent skill development initiatives?

- Does the company sponsor all or part of any costs?
- What are the potential career paths within the company for someone with my job title?
- To what jobs have people with my title risen in the company?

Corporate Culture

All companies have their own way of doing things—that's corporate culture. Not every corporate culture is for you.

- What is the company's mission? What are the company's goals?
- What approach does this company take to its marketplace?
- What is unique about the way this company operates?
- What is the best thing you know about this company? What is the worst thing you know about this company?
- How does the reporting structure work? What are the accepted channels of communication and how do they work?
- What kinds of checks and balances, reports, or other work-measurement tools are used in the department and company?
- What advice would you give me about fitting into the corporate culture—about understanding the way you do things here?
- Will I be encouraged or discouraged from learning about the company beyond my own department?

Company Growth and Direction

For those concerned about employment stability and career growth, a healthy company is mandatory.

- What expansion is planned for this department, division, or facility?
- What is your value proposition to prospective customers?
- When you lose a deal to whom do you lose it?
- What markets does the company anticipate developing?
- Does the company have plans for mergers or acquisitions?
- Currently, what new endeavors is the company actively pursuing?
- How do market trends affect company growth and progress? What is being done about them?

- What production and employee layoffs and cutbacks have you experienced in the last three years?
- What production and employee layoffs and cutbacks do you anticipate? How are they likely to affect this department, division, or facility?
- When was the last corporate reorganization? How did it affect this department?
- When will the next corporate reorganization occur? How will it affect this department?
- Is this department a profit center? How does that affect remuneration?

Negotiating Benefits

Once a base salary is on the table, and you've given it one shot at a bump upward, ask questions that give you more information with which to evaluate the opportunity. Then address benefits and other incentives. These can be an important compensation if the initial offer is lower than you wanted. For instance, you can ask about:

- A signing bonus
- A performance review after a specified number of days (90–120), followed by a raise
- A title promotion after a specified period
- A year-end bonus
- Stock options
- 401(k) and other investment-matching programs
- Compensation days for unpaid overtime/travel
- Life insurance
- Financial planning and assistance
- Paid sick leave
- Personal days off
- Profit sharing
- Vacation

How flexible are initial offers? The higher the position the more flexibility there is. Usually any offer is negotiable in some way. **What are the biggest mistakes?** Having an attitude of competition. This isn't about winning. It's about mutually agreeing and feeling good about how it was done.

Ron Weisinger, Principal Development, LINKS Consulting. Human Resources. 20 years' experience.

You can ask these questions over the phone, or request another meeting to review these points. I prefer the latter because you get to meet everyone as the new member of the team and the boss is buoyant because she can at last get back to work. These factors encourage agreement with reasonable requests, as might a *tiny* worry that you might walk and leave them back at square one.

You may get nothing more than the standard package, but you have nothing to lose by asking and everything to gain. Once the package is straightened out, come back to the base salary one last time: "I want the job, Charlie. I'm excited by the opportunity and working for you and joining the company, but is there anything we can do about the starting salary?" The answer to this question is going to determine what the final offer will be.

Best offer? Find out by asking, "Is this the best and final offer?" Adding, "I ask because I would like it in writing so that I can understand the specifics, e.g., bonus, benefits, vacation, sick leave, pension, probationary period. . . ."

Valentino Martinez, President, Martinez Group. Recruitment and University Relations. 38 years' experience.

Employment Obligations and Restrictions

Any verbal offer you accept is dependent on the offer being in writing and you being comfortable with what's in the employment agreement.

Pay careful attention to what the company will ask of you in signing the agreement. Employment contracts are legal documents designed to obfuscate and intimidate the neophyte. You can and should take the time to have it explained and then take it home and see if you agree with that interpretation; if in doubt, take it to any employment lawyer.

Your employment contract may include:

Assignment of Inventions

If you create anything during the period of your employment, the company may require you to turn it over. This may include work you do on your own time if it relates to your duties at the company.

Non-Disclosure Clauses

Companies will likely require that you not discuss company business with any outside source to prevent the competition from learning company secrets. The language is likely to be general and thus unfavorable to you. If you're concerned about this, try to get the language more specific.

Non-Compete Clauses

The company may want to restrict you from working for competitors after you leave the company. This can have a negative impact on your future career, since it restricts your employability. Try to make the language more specific.

Severance

Ask for a severance agreement. A month of salary for every year of employment or every $10,000 of salary is fairly standard. If you sign a non-compete agreement, require that your severance extend through the entire period of the non-compete.

Relocation

Relocation packages vary tremendously, and in recent years many companies have been cutting back on them. You want full moving services if at all possible, but even if you end up with a U-Haul truck, in addition to covering the cost of said truck and a few hundred dollars for incidentals, you can ask for everything from reimbursement for house-hunting trips to job search assistance for your spouse.

> **Final offer.** "I thank you for this offer. I am truly flattered that you think highly enough of me that you want me to join your company. The offer is very attractive; now I have to visit with my family and assess my gains and losses should I accept and make the move at this salary rate along with the entire compensation package."
>
> Valentino Martinez, President, Martinez Group. Recruitment and University Relations. 38 years' experience.

Accepting the Offer

The process of negotiating the offer may take some time, but when it's concluded be sure to mention how excited you are about the new job. Reply to the offer in a formal written letter. Begin composing your letter of resignation to your current employer as you prepare to step into a new phase of your career. Never resign your current position until you have an offer in writing, and when you do resign, do it gracefully. And leave without animus as you may well meet these people again one day.

> **Biggest mistake?** Not asking for more. No harm in asking. Be reasonable in what you want and don't backpedal. Make sure you are clear you want the job; you just want the elements of the offer to be acceptable.
>
> Nancy C. Anton, CPC. Talent Consultant, CIGNA. 20 years' experience.

Resources

- There is extensive advice about follow-up and negotiating an offer in the latest annual edition of *Knock 'em Dead: The Ultimate Job Search Guide.*
- Templates for follow-up, negotiation, acceptance, rejection, resignation, and other job search letters are available at *www.knockem dead.com.*

CHAPTER 14

STARTING ON THE RIGHT FOOT

All too often we join a new company and in an effort to make a good impression, we achieve the opposite.

I recently heard from an upwardly mobile marketing professional who was frustrated in her new job, "They hired me to innovate, and now I'm getting yessed to death, but there's no action!" How you behave when you first start work will determine your acceptance by management and by the team, your tenure, and your ultimate success with the company.

Here are some strategies that will help you avoid cranial-rectal inversion in your first months at that new job, and get this next step in your career started on the right foot.

Make a Positive First Impression

Your boss expects the same person who interviewed for the job to show up for work.

Bill Wilhelm, CPC. Executive Recruiter, Wilhelm and Associates, Inc. Industrial Sales and Manufacturing Management. 38 years' experience.

Never assume anything on a new job. Don't try to change the world before you know the way to the restroom. Your first task is to get to grips with your job, getting to know others who do this same job and the people whose work is affected by your work. Remember people's names, and go out of your way to smile and introduce yourself to everyone. Don't overlook clerical staff—it isn't courteous and allies here can always repay your cordiality down the line.

> **Learn the job,** the organization, the people. Show openness to feedback. Working extra hours as necessary without complaint. Form good relationships inside/outside your department.
>
> Ron Weisinger, Principal Development, LINKS Consulting. Human Resources. 20 years' experience.

Notice everyone's immediate work environment. In some companies a messy desk signifies an industrious, brilliant creative genius at work. In others it signifies a messy slob who's an embarrassment to the profession. Similarly, inquire about dress codes before you start.

As you get acclimatized over the first few days, you will begin to see the flow of work. Whatever the apparent madness you see in the early days at a new company, there is usually some very sound method behind it. The paychecks don't bounce, so the company's employees and officers must be doing something right. With this in mind, don't make comments about how things should be done, because no one will listen and some will take offense that the "newbie is a know-it-all." That just encourages some wise-ass to put you in your place.

> **Get clear direction on goals,** work as a team member, ask for regular feedback from your boss about how you are doing, and use the feedback to implement any changes that are needed. Teamwork and good relationships with others are critical as are delivering expected results.
>
> Marsha Connolly, Managing Partner, The New River Group. Certified Executive Coach. 30 years' experience.

You need time to get to know the company, its services, and its people. In turn, those people need time to get to know you. If you arrive and immediately begin reinventing the company, it will be seen as arrogance and is going to be taken as an insult. No one wants to hear your ideas or advice until they know your real value. First meetings are especially tricky. You'll be introduced and encouraged to speak up. By all means say that you're new and excited to join the team, that you have a lot to learn and hope you can ask for help as you learn your way around; beyond this say nothing.

> **Take notes,** make others feel what they say is important enough to write down. Say thank you to anyone who assists you, be appreciative of their time and input.
>
> Nancy C. Anton, CPC. Talent Consultant, CIGNA. 20 years' experience.

Start Small

> **Failure to communicate** is the major reason why things "don't work out." Do you know exactly what expectations they have of you? Do you know how your performance is being measured? Do you know the criteria to making a "keep" or "fire" decision?
>
> Bob Morris, Owner, Storage Placements. Data storage sales/marketing. 44 years' experience.

Take the time to get your feet on the ground, learn your way around, make friends, and absorb the culture. As you do this you'll see plenty of opportunities to make a difference with your presence. Prioritize them and start small, with each project meticulously conceived, planned, and implemented.

If you have ideas, the time to start introducing them is some time after the ninety-day probationary period, when you know:

- The names of everyone in the department
- How the department works and why it works that way

- How the company works and why it works that way
- Who's trustworthy and who isn't
- Management and other power players holding titles at least one and ideally two levels above you

> **Best things you can do?** Nail proficiency in your job first. Help pick up slack on a necessary but unpopular task. Do enough homework to ask intelligent questions. Make suggestions and recommendations that help move projects forward rather than attacking bedrock assumptions.
>
> Rick Kean, Consultant Emeritus, A. M. Hamilton, Inc. Staffing and training. 30+ years' experience.

When you have nailed job proficiency and the time is right to start making extra contributions, start with ideas for smaller projects—they are easier to sell, and help you build a foundation of credibility. Working on smaller projects first also helps you recognize and learn to finesse the hidden hierarchies that can torpedo any initiative.

Additionally, it doesn't hurt for your ideas, when you do introduce them, to be seen as part of a team effort. They will usually carry more initial weight when a member of that inner circle also has ownership. You don't lose credibility with their endorsement; you gain it.

At the same time as you are getting settled in and begin to feel accepted as a member of the team, management and your coworkers are looking carefully at how you function and informally accrediting you a status within the group. Their considerations evaluate:

- How well you know your job
- Whether you can be relied on to execute your duties in a professional way that is respectful of the work and responsibilities of others
- Whether you shoulder your share of the responsibility for a friendly, positive workplace
- How you make decisions, and whether they respect the business imperatives that everyone shares

- How you treat other people
- Whether you recognize others' contributions and give credit where it's due
- Whether you speak up for the team in meetings and defend its decisions
- Whether you respect the existing hierarchy within the team

You don't climb alone; no one does. You will do it most effectively with the support, encouragement, and camaraderie of similarly committed professionals, and as such we grow together. That's why the people at the top of every profession all know each other and have done so for years.

No one likes to be overwhelmed with genius, and the better you are, the more you have to work at your humility. Taking it slowly in the first ninety days will speed your acceptance by the group as a whole and allow you the time to recognize the real players amongst your peers. When it comes to establishing your credibility and visibility, the good news travels more slowly than the bad, but it does travel.

Teams accept you when you learn what makes this new team successful, and when you learn from them.

Perry Newman, CPC/CSMS. Executive Resume Writer/Career Coach.
25 years' experience.

The team rejects someone who has a condescending attitude. Don't be the guy who makes everyone feel like you were hired because they weren't doing anything right and you're there to fix it.

Michelle Hagans, Recruiter, Anu Resources Unlimited. IT and medical.
20+ years' experience.

CHAPTER 15

CLIMBING THE LADDER OF SUCCESS

Professional change is a constant in your life. If you want to make your dreams come true, you have to do things differently, and not just in your job search, but in the way you manage your career. Your new job is the golden opportunity to reinvent yourself and confirm a new trajectory for your professional life.

> **Maintain your digital footprint** and professional visibility: Update your LinkedIn profile to reflect new responsibilities!
>
> Olga Ocon, Executive Recruiter, Busch International. VP and CEO-level searches in high-tech. 15 years' experience.

The Leap of Faith

Believe in yourself, and back up that belief with action. Make this new job the turning point when you do a better job than you have ever done before *and* replace blind loyalty to the corporation with loyalty to your enlightened self-interest; and in the process this job will be more secure and increase your chances for professional growth.

You cannot afford to think that this job is the last stop in your career and that if you do a decent job your future will be secure.

Enlightened self-interest says to secure this job and pursue growth in a more mindful manner than before.

Protect Your Job and Boost Your Employability

Of all the skills you need to survive and prosper, *the very weakest of these, but the one you need to be strongest, is the skill of career management.* The moment you have settled into the new job and been accepted as a member of the team is the moment most people begin to coast, but coasting doesn't make the day go faster and doesn't help you live up to your dreams.

> **I miss out on promotions, why?** Because you have not done all of the things that position you for success and promotion, you have no one to blame but yourself.
>
> Grant Cooper, President, Careerpro of New Orleans. Strategic Resumes. 17 years' experience.

Build Your Core Competencies

Protect the job you have, for the security it brings and as a foundation for future growth. Every day, technology changes the skills you need to compete in the workplace, so if you are not consistently developing new skills, you are being paid for abilities that are rapidly becoming obsolete. Hone the *technical skills* of your job to perfection, until you are not only supremely competent but also better than you ever thought you could be.

To let your boss know you are committed to your job and to making a difference with your presence in the department, your conversation needs to make three points:

- I want to make a place for myself here, and to do that I need to be the best I can be.
- I'd like to hear any suggestions you have on skills that would make me more valuable to the team.

- These are skill sets I see as important in doing a stellar job, and I'd like to develop them by doing _____ [itemize the assignments that would develop these areas]. Your boss will make suggestions, and you should react positively to them. Lay out a plan of action, with realizable, step-by-step goals. Implement the advice, and follow up informally every 6–8 weeks to communicate both your commitment and progress; this establishes credibility and visibility where it counts. Do this and, apart from improving your professional competencies, you will have marked yourself out as someone who thinks, cares, and makes things happen. It's the first step in turning your boss into an ally.

Make Your Boss Your Ally

Protect the security of your job. Do the best job that you can, and ask your manager what you can do better and then implement the suggestions.

Rob Lockard, SPHR. HR Manager, The Centech Group. 9 years' experience.

Your boss has a profound influence over your ability to climb the ladder at the new company and build a successful career; you can help this happen by making your boss a fan and ally:

- Understand what's needed and deliver it on time and in the way your boss prefers.
- Make it accurate and what is requested rather than what you can get away with.
- Seek advice and accept constructive criticism gracefully.
- Share the credit you receive for work well done.
- Communicate clearly, professionally, honestly, and as often as your boss wants.
- Be a reliable team member in thought, word, and deed.
- Become *the most* reliable team member in thought, word, and deed.

- Consistently make your boss look good to others through your words and deeds.
- Thank your boss for either specific support on an endeavor or general encouragement.
- Never assume a job is complete when you hand it in. Be prepared to revise, edit, or recast your work.
- Increase your skills and expand your connectivity by volunteering for any interdepartmental projects or committees.
- Look for orphan projects that no one wants but that need to be done.

Avoid doing the following:

- Don't over-commit yourself to the point that your performance suffers.
- Never display disloyalty. If you're seeking a promotion your boss should know and be part of the program.
- Ensure by your actions that others within your department know of your loyalty to them and to the department's goals.
- Never criticize your boss to other employees.
- Don't be a Cassandra: No one wants to listen to the employee who's predicting the imminent collapse of civilization. Even if the company or the industry is headed into some difficult times, be a positive influence. This doesn't mean you should stick your head in the sand and get caught job hunting with three hundred of your closest colleagues: Stick to the larger career management strategy we have discussed.
- Too often departments take refuge in a narrow separatism that counterpoises their interests to everyone else's. Sales says, "Those people in Accounting are obstructionist bean-counters who get in the way of the people who bring in the money," while the accountants say, "Sales are a bunch of wild-eyed maniacs who don't understand the practical realities; it's our work that makes sure the paychecks don't bounce."

Don't buy into this mindset. Instead, respect and show interest in the roles others play. This will increase your credibility, visibility, and frame of reference for how the money-making machinery of business works.

Together, these attitudes and actions will cement a good relationship with your boss and could well lead to your boss also becoming your mentor, and being personally involved in your growth and success.

Find Mentors, Become a Mentor

Mentors, more experienced professionals you admire and from whom you can learn, can accelerate your professional growth. These mentor-acolyte relationships have been an integral part of successful careers throughout the ages.

This relationship is not necessarily between you and your boss, although your boss can be a mentor. Rather, it's a relationship between professionals of different experience levels who share a common commitment to professional excellence. Your mentor will guide you through those aspects of your profession that you haven't yet mastered. You enter into these relationships hoping for the Zen-master relationship, where you are given useful directions and the occasional whack up the side of the head that helps you align the wisdom. In return you offer your help and best efforts to your mentor in any way or circumstance in which she can use it. Remember:

- Mentors aren't like lovers. You can have more than one at a time.
- Although age and wisdom don't always go together, it is better to find a mentor older than you, because they'll have skills you don't and the wisdom of greater experience. You need both.
- Mentor-acolyte relationships can introduce you to your mentor's network.
- Look for mentors both within and without your area of subject-matter expertise, both within your company and in the larger pond of your local professional community.

- Let the relationship develop naturally, over time. You might work together, have known each other, and get on well for some time before you say, "I want to learn everything you know. I want you to teach me, and in return I will stand at your side, have your back, and do anything I can to return this favor."
- When you see someone coming along who seems truly dedicated to long-term professional success, you too should become a mentor.

> **Find a mentor, be a mentor.** I'm a big proponent of pairing up with someone from another generation—Gen Ys and Baby Boomers make a particularly good pair.
>
> Allison Farber Cheston, Career Advisor, Allison Cheston & Associates. Author, *In the Driver's Seat: Work-Life Skills for Young Adults.* 28 years' experience.

The Vacuum Theory

Avoid that career-killing phrase, "Not in my job description." By working on your *technical* and *transferable skills* and making the *professional values* a vibrant part of your *professional self,* you have positioned yourself to make contributions above, below, and beyond your job level, because you are genuinely engaged in making a difference for good with your presence.

A former boss of mine applied something I've come to call the Vacuum Theory of Growth: Walking down the hall one day, he saw a gum wrapper on the floor. He bent and picked it up. "Only two people would do that: the janitor and maybe the president. They both know who I am," he said, smiling.

This guy executed his job with utter excellence; he volunteered for and was involved in every initiative for growth that the company had going, was always one of the first three people in the office, and would smilingly lend a hand to anyone who needed it. He also looked for vacuums, necessary jobs that no one wanted to do. Consequently, he had allies everywhere and at every level, and he always knew everything that happened in that company before it happened.

Once you are more than adequately competent with the essential *technical skills* of your job, look around for opportunity. Then start sucking up extra responsibility by doing those necessary, extra things that no one else wants to do, 'cause it's "not my job." The result is enhanced credibility, visibility with the people who count, and a power base for future growth. When you do the right things for the right reasons, you always benefit from the effort; sometimes not immediately, but you always do benefit.

The Vacuum Theory is an expression of motivation: Do your job well first, then help others whenever and however you can; do the jobs others won't and make a visible difference with your presence every day.

Making the Inner Circle

Credibility, flexibility, the right attitude, the confidence that you can be counted on and that you have your coworkers' backs. Are you someone others want to be with? If you are, good things will always happen for you.

Nancy C. Anton, CPC. Talent Consultant, CIGNA. 20 years' experience.

The inner circle is where your job is safest and where the plum assignments, raises, and promotions live. *It's where you become visible to the power players two, three, and four levels above you.* Add the following three commitments to everything you have learned so far and you will gain the attention of, and acceptance by, the people who make up the inner circles within your department and company.

1. Commit to the success of every project, every team, and every department with which you are involved. Secure this job and create a launch pad for growth.
2. Get behind every project leader, no matter who it is and what your relationship may have been with her up to this point.

You work to make both the project and that project leader a success. *Your efforts are always noticed by the people who matter.*

3. Give your best on every assignment, no matter how undesirable, because you know that taking the rough with the smooth is part of achieving success. *The real players, the members of the inner circle, know this and respect it in others.*

When you polish your *technical skills*, support everything you do with *transferable skills*, and make sure your judgments are informed by sound *professional values*, you become a highly desirable employee. When you pursue your work with *commitment* and *enlightened self-interest*, you will be welcomed into the inner circles of your department and company. This will lead to expanding your connectivity beyond the company, because the members of your immediate inner circle are *the people who are most committed and also the best-connected to the profession beyond your company.*

> **I want to succeed.** You get into the inner circle when people, like you, trust you, respect you, and want to be around you. Volunteer to do essential things that many of your peers consider below them. Speak up and contribute in a low-key positive manner.
>
> Perry Newman, CPC/CSMS. Executive Resume Writer/Career Coach. 25 years' experience.

Inner Circles Beyond Your Company

Beyond the inner circles of your department and your company lie those of your profession. Becoming connected to the most committed and best-connected people in your industry can have many long-term benefits, not the least of which will be increasing your visibility and opportunities.

Professional association membership and active involvement is the smartest career strategy you can initiate to achieve wide professional connectivity. You will keep current with professional issues and new skills, and you will get to know and be known by everyone who is anyone in your profession. Make involvement in association activities something you do as a matter of course every month.

How to Pursue and Win a Promotion

Your next step up the ladder doesn't come automatically as a result of being in the inner circle; but it positions you to make that step.

What is the smartest way to win promotions? Work harder than others—turn out an exceptional product, treat everyone, regardless of rank, with the same kindness; *always* do more than expected.

Sean Koppelman, President, The Talent Magnet. Advertising, beauty, and entertainment. 16 years' experience.

The work on that promotion, however, starts when you join the company. Spend the first few months figuring out the way things work. Once you understand the culture, get up to speed with all your job's deliverables, and know who's who in your department and why, it's time to start strategizing your next step up the promotion ladder.

Promotions come as a result of hard work, credibility, visibility, and a plan of action to gain the required qualifications. *You get hired based on credentials, not potential,* and *you get promoted when you are a known quantity* within the company.

This is how you win promotions:

1. Review the *TJD* you did for the job you now hold. Do you have superior skills in all the areas required for this job? If so, go to the next step; if not, take the time to bring these skills up to par: This makes your employment more secure.
2. When you are ready, identify the next logical step up your chosen professional ladder, collect 6–10 job postings for your target job title, and do a *TJD*.

3. Identify the *gaps* between the skills you have and the skills you need to qualify you for that next job. Flagging missing skills and experience gives you a professional development program to pursue.

4. Identify ways you can build these skills within company activities and on your own initiative.

5. Talk to your boss about your desire to gain these new skills and experience. Explain that you want to work toward this job over time by developing the skills it demands. If the next step is your boss's job, succession planning is something most managers understand: You can't go for a promotion until you have someone trained behind you to take your place. Stepping forward to help yourself can also help your boss climb upward.

6. Model yourself on people who do this job successfully. Look for a mentor who is doing this job.

Moving Up

When a position opens up, a company normally looks within and then goes outside for talent. This outside talent comes armed with resumes that carefully focus on the experience and abilities they can bring to the job. You will prepare in the same way, first creating a resume targeted to this job and then preparing for interviews just as you would with another company.

It is easier to climb the ladder within a company where you are a known quantity and have the kind of sterling reputation you have worked to achieve. You will throw your hat in the ring when opportunities arise and be patient if you don't win first time out.

I miss out on promotions, why? Seek critical feedback when you don't. Difficult conversations are often pushed aside with the "keep trying" retort. Don't let [your boss] off easy: "I know this is hard, but I really want to know what is holding me back." Using that advice is crucial to your development within an organization.

Karen McGrath, PHR. Talent Acquisition Manager, Enterprise Rent-A-Car. 22 years' experience.

However, your commitment is to MeInc's success, and a time may come when you believe this next step is not possible with your current company.

If and when this situation arises, you are armed with greatly enhanced skills, the professional credibility and visibility that should now constitute a truly valid professional brand. You are an active member of at least your regional professional community, and you have a resume targeted to a job that you have the skills and experience to excel at. Plus you have a database of companies and contacts within them that you established in your last job search and added to in this job. Pulling all this together, you have the time, tools, skills, connections, and knowledge to make this next strategic career move on your own timetable.

Keeping your short- and long-term goals in focus every day encourages you to do all the grunt work that brings them to fruition.

Resources

Knock 'em Dead: Breaking Into Management and *Knock 'em Dead: Professional Communication* are both available at *www.knockemdead .com.*

CHAPTER 16

LIFETIME CAREER MANAGEMENT—
ISSUES AND STRATEGIES

You have been taught to think of career management as choosing one thing you can do and settling down to it for a lifetime. You hang on with ten fingers and ten toes, and if you should lose one of them, well golly-gosh you hang on with nine, because that's the way it's done. Your loyalty will be rewarded with job and financial security and steady professional growth. This delightful fairy tale ends with a comfortable retirement, featuring a home you own and a cabin at the lake.

Despite this being a pile of rocking-horse droppings, nothing has come along to replace it. As people have lost jobs and professions because of technological change and economic recession, cutting-edge career advice has said that change happens and change is for the best, and bless your heart, we're getting rid of these stinky old bad jobs and replacing them with bright shiny new ones. All you have to do is: choose one *other* thing you can do, settle down to it for the rest of your life, and hang on with ten fingers. . . .

How should I manage my career differently? Be less resistant to new ideas and embrace personal growth.

Karen McGrath, PHR. Talent Acquisition Manager, Enterprise Rent-A-Car. 22 years' experience.

There is another way of looking at career management. If you don't adapt, your professional life is going to sputter along from job to job and career to career, with all the financial dislocation and soul-wrenching self-doubt that job change and career change bring on in everyone who goes through them.

We typically start to work in our teens and theoretically retire at sixty-five, although the boomer generation knows this will not be economically feasible because of the effect that regular and increasingly violent economic swings have had on retirement plans. This picture of financial insecurity won't improve for younger generations, especially while corporate and political greed happily continue to export jobs overseas to further enrich the wealthiest 1 percent, who still manage to convince a majority of Americans that while they do this, they also share the interests, concerns, and values of working people.

The reality you face is that constant change in your professional life threatens your ability to achieve success. This is why you must embrace a practical approach to lifetime career management that focuses on enlightened self-interest.

Where Do You Want to Be at Retirement?

Thinking about what you want to do for a career right now and which job you should pursue next is wrong. You should start by thinking about your endgame: where you want to be and what you want your life to be like, and work backwards from there.

This has to go beyond fine dining and a glossy magazine's description of the ideal consumer. You need to be thinking about quality of life, about the career paths and effort that can realistically be expected to deliver your dreams. This will include the focused pursuit of what you will come to see as your corporate *core career*, accompanied, depending on your inclinations, by the pursuit of parallel *entrepreneurial* and *dream careers*. Imagine the life you want, and are prepared to work to achieve. You can dream of being the president of the company, the president of your own company, of becoming an artist, writer, or musician, because this is America and we are a nation that allows people to reinvent themselves.

But dreams don't materialize out of thin air. You start with a dream and then determine concrete goals, and from those goals establish a plan of action that takes you toward them step-by-step. Goals can be achieved when you invest yourself *intelligently* in their achievement.

You Have the Time, If You Have the Commitment

Every day that you wake up on the right side of the grass you are ahead of the game and one day closer to achieving your goals.

Your career doesn't have to be about either/or choices: "I want to be president of the company" and "I want to be president of my own company" aren't mutually exclusive. You can realistically have multiple career goals and expect to achieve a number of them: goals for climbing the corporate ladder, for having an antique shop or your own white-water rafting company, for writing that book or having a solo exhibition of your new sculpture at MOMA.

The parallel career strategy, which encourages the pursuit of personal endeavor, is built upon the firmest foundations available to you—the creation of a stable *core career* with upward mobility—so first we need to talk about making the right long-term decisions for your *core career*. Both career change and career choice are complex issues that require understanding and careful thought.

The Foundations for Smart Career Change and Career Choice

If you want to change jobs, talk to a recruiter in your field. **If you want to change careers,** do not talk to a recruiter, talk to people in that industry.

Maynard G. Charron, President, Paper Industry Recruitment. 30+ years' experience.

We are going to talk about career change, then career choice. If you are at the start of your working life, don't skip ahead. You need a frame of reference for what your future will hold, and many of the strategies used in career change will be the same ones you use in career choice.

Long-term success starts by securing your corporate *core career*: *Become the best you can be to secure the job you have today and to land the job you want tomorrow.* Reinvent your *professional self* in the practical ways we have discussed throughout *Secrets & Strategies*, and you will secure your job and be positioned for the plum assignments, raises, and promotions that await the truly committed. This is the smartest path to job security and professional growth, and you know it makes sense.

Nevertheless, job change happens—sometimes planned, sometimes not—and it is rarely easy. It takes careful planning and execution to keep the cash flow uninterrupted, but now you have the awareness and the tools in hand to execute strategic career moves within your chosen profession. You don't have to be caught unawares by a layoff. You can become more informed, better connected, and plan your moves. With a career management database in place and relevant social networks developed, the moves can be made on a considered basis and at a time of your choosing, when you decide there is no further opportunity to move toward your goals with a current employer, or outside forces tell you that your job is no longer secure.

The Perils of Career Change

A career change is a much more intimidating affair than a job change within your chosen profession because it can cause extensive financial and emotional dislocation unless unfailingly planned in advance. The worst time to change careers is when you are out of work. Having been caught in an economic downturn, you are short of cash and the bills are piled nose-high. The competition is fiercer than you have ever faced in the new target profession because you are up against candidates with experience in that profession.

It is far wiser to plan career change well ahead of time and to make the shift when the economy is good and there are more job opportunities than candidates. But even with the most careful planning in the world, this won't always be your choice. If you want to change careers but don't know where to start, there is a free database at *www .knockemdead.com* that allows you to match degrees with careers.

Best time for career change is when you've carefully built a new social network that has excellent contacts in your intended field.

Grant Cooper, President, Careerpro of New Orleans. Strategic Resumes. 17 years' experience.

Overcoming Obstacles with a Career Change

I recently helped a guy having problems with a mid-career shift. Late thirties, and thirteen unhappy years in sales/marketing, led to career reappraisal and a return to university to gain a Finance MBA.

His job search was bogged down and he diagnosed the problem as, "no job offers because of my inability to answer specific questions about *why the career change*." I told him getting his new career moving would take more than a few snappy answers to tough interview questions. In fact his problems stemmed from a combination of factors.

It wasn't that he hadn't yet latched onto the most convincing arguments to justify his career shift. While this was certainly a part of the problem, understanding, believing, and demonstrating that he understood the deliverables of the target job and its role within the department, and that he understood how the industry worked and why it worked this way, and finally why his prior professional experience was actually a distinct benefit to the new employer, was a bigger and more important challenge. Translation: He had to learn to build the bridges that would enable the employer to say, "Sure, walk on over."

Your success at landing job interviews and then acing them in a career–change job search will dramatically improve with greater understanding of your target job's function and the world it inhabits.

Defining the New Job, Understanding the New Profession
Your current job and your target job in the new profession have two things in common: They exist to *anticipate, prevent, and solve*

problems in an area of specific technical expertise within a department of similarly talented professionals who collectively perform a specialized function in helping a company make money. Understand the role this new job plays in contributing to the department, the problems it is there both to prevent and to solve, and ultimately how it supports the company's profitability, and you will see what employers look for when they interview potential employees. You'll get a picture of your new target job by executing a *TJD*, then doing a *gap* analysis: Flag the skills you need to build, and the information you need to gather on how to build these skills.

You will also begin to think about the job titles in this target profession that can explain the day-to-day deliverables of the job and its challenges, and the behavioral profiles for your target job title. The people who can help you most are the same high-value job titles you will need to develop for networking and job search when you start pursuing the new job.

> **Career Change.** Transferable skills are the very first thing looked at by a recruiting/HR professional evaluating if a candidate can make "the leap" from one industry or line of business to another.
>
> Rob Lockard, SPHR. HR Manager, The Centech Group. 9 years' experience.

Contacts you make in the new industry can tell you about the role of the job in contributing to profitability, the problems it exists to solve, and its role within the department. They can tell you about the *technical skills* required and how they are applied in the work; and which *transferable skills* and *professional values* are most important in that job and how they are applied. For example, *multitasking* will naturally be an important skill. But what are the primary activities of the new job, and when do they occur during the working day? And what other important but repetitive activities must also be scheduled and completed during the working week?

Use Your Networks

Your best bet for learning more about the day-to-day challenges of a target job in a new profession is to talk with people working in the desired area within the target industry/profession; *people with similar educational and work backgrounds, and ideally people who have already made a similar shift successfully* and who hold, have held, or whose jobs require them to work with, your Target Job Title.

Your alumni association will be a useful resource for this, as will a professional association related to the new job, and your social networking sites. With all these resources you can search for members:

- Working in the target profession
- Working in the target profession and sharing a similar educational background
- Working in the target profession who have made a similar transition

This is where you need to tap your personal and professional networks, as previously discussed.

Apart from people who share your transitional experience from one profession to another, people up and down the promotional ladder in that job (the high–value networking titles) and profession can all offer worthwhile advice.

You will also want answers to the following:

- How has your prior professional background in _____ paid off in your new profession?
- How has it helped you better understand _____ to the benefit of the corporation?
- What special insights have you gained that make you more productive?
- Why do you think this combined background of _____ and _____ is helpful to an employer?

Talk to your network contacts about how the target job fits into the department and contributes to the company's bottom line. This means researching the problems and challenges this job exists to *anticipate, prevent, and solve,* as well as the *technical skills* required and the way productivity is measured.

> **Make it easy for them to hire you.** Recruiters with carefully defined criteria are reading your resume. Put yourself in their shoes and give them the information they're looking for in a document or web page that's easy to read and digest. Make it easy for them to assess your "fit" for the position and corporate culture.
>
> Meg Guiseppi, C-level Executive Job Search Coach, Executive Career Brand. 20+ years' experience.

The answers you receive are puzzle pieces that together will give you a clear picture of what interviewers are looking for. Aside from any relevant academic qualifications, with the *transferable skills* and *professional values*, you already possess many of the tools that are needed to be successful in the new target job.

It will take time to make the contacts and gather the insights you need to fully understand the target job in its day-to-day professional context. The knowledge you gather will help you build the bridges that connect your past experience with your new direction and the ability to lead your interviewers across them.

It's Your Resume, Stupid

Resumes not only open doors for you, they give the employer a focus and road map for the interview; in a very real way, *the understanding of your target job expressed in your resume sets the tone for the interview.* You started with a *TJD* of the new job, identified specific skills that need to be developed, and finally researched what the true role and deliverables of the job are. Now, with a complete understanding of the job, you can build a resume better focused on those deliverables. This will help you land interviews and enter them with a competitive edge.

. . . And Your Job Search Tactics

A career change job search takes longer than a regular one because it first requires research and networking to understand the job, and then to coordinate a search. Implementation of a job search should follow the plan of attack laid out earlier. As you cannot rely on your resume to deliver interviews, your attack will feature a strong emphasis on direct research and high-value title networking.

When your job search involves career change, winning a job offer will never depend on the answers to a handful of interview questions; it will depend instead on your ability to communicate your understanding of the target job's deliverables and *why* and *how* you can deliver on them.

While I don't recommend making a career change during a recession, we are a huge economy and there are plenty of jobs out there, and when you go about it with the right preparation and determination, you can succeed.

Be Smart, Choose a Practical Core Career

With all its lack of security, a traditional *core career* is still the most secure route to middle-class success. When you are considering career choice for the first time, or want to change careers but don't know what you want to change to, it makes sense to look at your options with a clear head. There is no real job security in traditional career paths, but pursued with the *Knock 'em Dead* plan of attack, your job can become more secure and you will be more credible and more visible to your professional world.

It's critical to be an active participant in your career, and not a passenger! Many of the jobs that will exist in ten years don't exist today, and on the flip side, you could become a dinosaur if you don't keep up!

Allison Farber Cheston, Career Advisor, Allison Cheston & Associates. Author, *In the Driver's Seat: Work-Life Skills for Young Adults.* 28 years' experience.

All career management advice to date tells you to find your passion, find your bliss, find something you love, and stick with it until you achieve success. That's not always practical. If you want to give it a shot, go ahead, but don't stay too long at the party; entering the professional work force at the entry-level is easy enough up until twenty-five, but leave it two or three more years and employers begin to get leery. Leave it too long and getting a foothold in a professional career can be very difficult. If you bear with me, I can offer you a successful *core career* and a real shot at living your dreams.

The experts tell us to expect three or more careers over a worklife, which averages out to around fifteen years per career, unless you become successful in one and stay with it.

> **Stay on the headhunters' radar.** Get to know good recruiters when you aren't looking for a job. Help them as a resource whenever possible.
>
> George Olmstead. Managing Partner, Olmstead Lynch & Kreutz. Senior management recruitment. 30 years' experience.

Your needs/desires—the things you find worthwhile in life—will evolve as you age, and you will probably experience significant changes in these areas every 7–10 years. Because the metrics say that no job is secure and psychological research says that whatever rings bells for you today might not have the same relevance a few years down the road, career choice shouldn't necessarily be about finding your passion, although it's preferable if you can make a living doing things you enjoy. A more practical approach that responds to the realities of the new world of work is possible: The work you do dictates the money you earn every week, and this dictates the quality of life you experience and the things you are able to do when you are not working; and this has an impact on every day of your life, for the rest of your life. *Core career* choice should be based on pragmatism, and it can afford to be when a *core career* isn't the sum of your life, but part of a more intelligent approach to career management that is in tune with the times *and supports your need for success and ongoing financial security.* While *core career* choice should certainly take into account personal preferences, it should not be made in the belief that this career will lead to lifelong security or that it will satisfy all your needs for today and always. Later on in the chapter you'll learn how your *core career* can become the launch pad for both successful *entrepreneurial* and *dream careers.*

Smart core career choice should take into account skills, aptitudes, and preferences; and having come up with a short list based on these considerations, you should also consider:

- The projected health of the industry sector
- The projected growth of the target job(s)
- The relative flexibility offered by that degree/job/industry combination in allowing you to change jobs and professions in the future

An industry sector/profession with healthy growth projections will deliver more job opportunities and better professional growth in good times and bad.

Within the profession/industry sector(s) under evaluation, you should consider the projected health of target jobs. Jobs with high projected growth potential—20-plus percent growth over the next decade is considered pretty healthy—are better than jobs with little or no projected growth.

> **Industries like Healthcare,** Insurance, Accounting, Non-Profit, and Education tend to place less emphasis on age and are happy to see someone with a rich employment industry. Human Resources as a discipline (especially due to a sensitivity/knowledge of age discrimination) also sees many more people employed closer to retirement age than others.
>
> Sean Koppelman, President, The Talent Magnet. Advertising, beauty, and entertainment. 16 years' experience.

The absolute number of people holding that job title today and on which the growth projections are based is also important: A projected

20 percent growth rate on a job that already has 3 million people holding that job title suggests greater security than a job with a projected 20 percent growth rate based on 35,000 people.

What Comes First, the Career Choice or the Degree?

Paying for college is expensive, so you want to make the smartest choices that also offer the greatest flexibility for changing jobs and careers later in your professional life.

1. Learn about the growth industries, the high-growth jobs within them, the academic credentials required for entry, and the credentials suggested for an accelerated start.
2. Cross-reference the academic requirements for the job(s) and career path(s) under consideration with the other jobs and careers people with these same degrees have pursued successfully.

Secrets & Strategies does not address cross-referencing of career paths and degree programs. However, at *www.knockemdead.com* I have a database that houses information on *all major four–year degree programs*, the career directions that people successfully pursue with that degree, and some useful links with which to pursue your inquiries.

Based on this input, and having taken full advantage of any counseling and career choice/aptitude testing available to you, it will be possible to make considered career choices based on opportunity for job security and professional growth.

For Career-Changers Examining Their Options

If you are already working in the professional world, the steps will be the same, but the order could be different. Begin by examining the doors that your degree could help you open and researching the health of the industry sectors in which these jobs reside. The questions then tumble out about the difficulty of locating all this information. Go to the Career Advice pages at *www.knockemdead.com*, then click on *Secrets & Strategies* where you will find a Where The Jobs Are Appendix, designed to complement this chapter (we actually ran out of pages). This will give you an objective review of the healthiest growth sectors in the U.S. economy for the foreseeable future, and many of the highest-growth jobs in those sectors, as well as links for finding out more about each of these jobs.

Career Choice and the Bigger Picture

> **Build financial security,** become known and respected in your field, and develop separate sources of work that can provide additional streams of income. Build new skills, create alternate relationships, support networks, and future opportunities.
> Plan and prepare for the day when you run your own business, eliminating dependency on an employer.
>
> Marsha Connolly, Managing Partner, The New River Group. Certified Executive Coach. 30 years' experience.

If you want to increase your chances of financial independence, your *core career* is just that: central to your success, but not the only path to its achievement. Pursue your *core career* with dedication for the rewards that success can bring you, but your *core career* also functions as the training ground for your pursuit of parallel *dream* and *entrepreneurial careers.*

The Building Blocks of Career Success and Personal Fulfillment

There are three paths to building a successful life for yourself:

1. **Core Career:** Building a career working for companies that pay salary and offer vacations, benefits, and some degree of professional growth.

Core Career Reality: There is no real job security, but it is still the most secure route to middle-class success.

2. **Dream Career:** It can be anything you want, from writing the Great American Novel to becoming a cellist in the Vienna Philharmonic.

 Dream Career Reality: A dream career should be something that gives you joy, puts *the juice back in your life*. By definition hard to achieve, it should not replace a steady means of making a living; besides, that *core career* has all kinds of valuable lessons that will help you realize your dreams. If you hope to live that dream, you have to turn it into realizable goals and a plan of action: actual steps you can begin to take to get you from here to there.

 Everything starts with a dream, and stays that way over many years as you work steadily toward it. It ceases being a dream the moment you start to make money from it: At that moment you become a creative entrepreneur and your *dream career* transforms into an *entrepreneurial career*. It happens, and if you are the creative type, which all entrepreneurs and businesspeople are, you'll soon latch onto another dream, knowing you crave the juice it brings to your life.

3. **Entrepreneurial Career:** When you work for yourself, there's no employer between you and the money. The closer you get to the source of money, to bringing it steadily in your own front door, the closer you are to economic security.

What can I do differently? Profit prevails over all and loyalty is nonexistent. The best way to ensure success is to be an entrepreneur and have greater control of your destiny.

Perry Newman, CPC/CSMS. Executive Resume Writer/Career Coach.
25 years' experience.

Entrepreneurial Career Reality: More businesses fail than succeed. Most entrepreneurs rush into a business without preparation or skills, and give up their entrepreneurial dreams after that first failure. Almost all successful entrepreneurs have experienced one or more failures before they achieve success.

Your Core Career Is the Cradle of Life for Your Dreams

With all its uncertainties, your *core career* is still the surest path to security and success, and while it shouldn't be your only path in such an insecure world, there is a trade-off: Use your day-to-day *core career* experience wisely and you will find that it can be a complete educational program for the launch of successful *dream* and *entrepreneurial careers*.

I funded three behavioral studies a few years ago that looked at the *transferable skills* and *professional values* needed for long-term career success in *core, dream, and entrepreneurial* careers. There was already some consensus in the professional community about the skills, behaviors, and values it takes to be successful in the corporate (*core career*) world, but no comparative studies for *core* vs. *entrepreneurial* and *dream careers*. It was done by a behavioral psychologist of standing in the corporate world and with academic oversight from a New England university.

I was pleasantly unsurprised when the study found that the *transferable skills* and *professional values* are *equally applicable* to success in all three career paths. This has some powerful implications: *Because the professional values and transferable skills*—true to their name—*encourage success in all three career paths, the pursuit of these parallel careers and the skills vital to your core career mutually reinforce one another.*

Applying the *transferable skills* and *professional values* in the pursuit of that dream/entrepreneurial career not only increases your odds of achieving your dream, it further refines those skills and widens your frame of reference in the context of your core career, thus spelling greater core career success even if the dream doesn't pan out as quickly or as well as you might have wished. This should make you look at your *core career* in a new light; every day will be full of

OJT (on-the-job-training) opportunities to learn the lessons of business and apply them to your own pursuits, your own enlightened self-interest.

It's Good to Have Goals in Life

At the beginning of the book I suggested pulling out some of your dreams from under the bed and making them part of your life, part of your identity. The more complete the vision of your future, the more clearly you can identify and define the many small steps, taken day-by-day, that bring your vision to life. New paths down which you can pursue success and personal fulfillment represent long-term commitments that probably won't spring into bloom this coming spring. They will take time, sometimes years, before they bear fruit, but their pursuit will enrich your life in the process.

Your wants, needs, and dreams will change as the years pass. What seemed a worthwhile pursuit in your twenties changes to something new in your thirties, and so on. Most people who try to pursue their dreams try once in their teens, twenties, or thirties and, failing, vow never to make the same mistake again. Successful entrepreneurs, however, take their knocks, lick their wounds, own their mistakes, and do better next time; and there always *is* a next time until they achieve success; they simply don't quit, no matter how long it takes.

If you learn from your mistakes and commit yourself to achieving your dreams no matter how long it takes, that crazy idea that didn't work out in your teens or twenties shouldn't prevent you from trying again in your thirties with a new idea, or in your forties, fifties, and beyond. Laura Ingalls Wilder, the author of *Little House on the Prairie*, didn't start writing till she was sixty-five years old. My old friend Ross, who drew Mickey for Disney and is one of the last living animators to have worked on *Fantasia* back in the nineteen thirties, is completely engaged in a new philanthropic business venture at ninety-two.

It is okay to have multiple goals in life, because if you buy into the plan, *you have the tools to bring them to life and you have the time if you have the commitment*, and start today.

A Successful Career Is Not a Sprint

A successful career is a marathon, not a sprint; so whatever your goals, the sooner you start toward them the better. Begin studying for that degree or that real estate license, take that painting class, or read that book on what makes entrepreneurs tick or how small businesses succeed and why they fail. Do it, because you *can* do it.

You can make the time. If you don't have time, I can give you, right now, a gift of five hours every day to invest in making your life a richer experience: Stop watching five hours of TV every day (that's how much the average American watches). Stop watching your life whiz by on the screen, stop training to be a good consumer and an obedient drone. Instead, invest some or all of that time in you—*in your life*—in MeInc and the realization of your dreams.

Look for stepping-stones to take you from where you stand today to where you want to stand tomorrow; and look for connectivity between how the actions that can help you achieve goals in your corporate *core career* might also encourage the steps you take toward an *entrepreneurial* or *dream career*.

Stepping-Stones and Calendars

I once knew a young man who worked as a headhunter—not a very glamorous job three decades ago. He was relatively successful but unfulfilled (he dreamed of being a writer or an actor). He wanted to change careers but had to keep paying the bills. What did he do? He looked for stepping-stones to get away from the front line of sales. After some thought he decided that becoming a sales trainer looked like a promising option, so he started to help get new sales employees up-to-speed with his current employer.

Planning Strategic Career Moves

> **Career changes are best taken** incrementally and taken during times when financial, professional, and personal obligations allow time for exploration and experimentation.
>
> Marsha Connolly, Managing Partner, The New River Group. Certified Executive Coach. 30 years' experience.

He used what he already had (*technical skills*), sharing his knowledge (*teamwork* and *communication skills*) as stepping-stones to get where he wanted to go. Becoming a trainer would get him off the front line of sales into another area of professional expertise and give him new *technical skills* to transfer from company to company and even from industry to industry. Plus the training work would have him up and performing in front of an audience, helping his stage presence as an actor (and increasing his credibility and visibility*)*.

Skill Development

He really strove to develop great training skills, and he always looked for connectivity between his core career goals and his dream of one day writing the Great American Novel and never working another day in his life. The more he understood the mechanics of professional success, the more he saw patterns emerge, and the more connectivity he found between seemingly disparate activities, the more opportunities he saw for advancing toward his goals. For example, he saw the absence of training manuals (*creativity* based on *technical skills* and being a *team player*) and how they could increase productivity with new employees.

He wanted to write, and knew from his studies (*commitment, determination*) that any writing would help in learning how to craft powerful sentences. So he wrote any manual, any time, for any employer he worked for (*communication skills*). It served multiple career goals:

- It branded him as someone thoroughly *committed*.
- It branded him as someone with a special sauce to bring to the table.

- It increased his professional credibility.
- It increased his visibility by widening his contacts and sphere of influence.
- It developed his *writing* skills.

Stepping-Stones

Two jobs, many manuals, and five years later, he landed with a franchiser of employment service companies as a sales and management trainer. Committed to succeeding, he continued to learn everything he could about his profession as a trainer (*technical skills*) and about the world of employment. He found a great mentor and helped the mentor in return.

Within a year he was being recruited for other franchise companies in other industries (brand recognition); but he stayed and shortly became Director of Training and Development as his boss moved up to VP (*inner circle*). Over the years he had built career stepping-stones for himself, using a horizontally oriented career that could cross industry lines (more *security* and more opportunities for *professional growth*).

It Takes Time

How should I manage my career differently? Keeping a road map [of the steps to reach your goals] will act like a compass and give you both direction and impetus to move forward and build momentum.

Valentino Martinez, President, Martinez Group. Recruitment and University Relations. 38 years' experience.

Stepping-stones take you from where you are to where you want to be, but it takes time. This young man had bills to pay and now a family coming along but he still dreamed of being a novelist or an actor (dream careers). He wasn't either, but he'd walked toward a job he was very good at and polished his writing and performance skills along the way. He was indeed much happier, more secure, and more successful.

Stepping-stones take you across the river from where you feel stuck to where you dream of being. This young man had other dreams too. He dreamed of working for himself. He'd tried three times before but the dreams hadn't worked out (*entrepreneurial, determination*). As a trainer, part of his job was *writing* training manuals; what was a *dream* avocation had grown into a core career *technical skill*. He wrote dozens of manuals to hone his writing skills, and he wrote novels as he sat in airports or hotels on business trips (*multitasking, time management, communication,* and *organization*). He got a book published five years after starting this new approach to life and career management, but twenty years after he'd first thought of himself as wanting to be a writer (*dream career* becomes *entrepreneurial career*). Now, twenty-five years later, he's written twelve books, has his own company, and is still nowhere near the end of his half-century work life. Over time, pursuit of those *dreams* enriched his *core career* skills and employability; after twenty years' pursuit, they started making money and gave birth to a real *entrepreneurial career* that became a stable *core career*.

Sometimes You Fall Short, and It Ain't So Bad

Like the guy in the story I've just told you, maybe you'll never make all your long-term goals; maybe you'll fall a little short—like he did.

He wanted to write novels; instead he unintentionally became a non-fiction writer. He never became an actor either, but pursuing the acting dream put juice in his life and helped him achieve success with the platform skills he needed as a trainer. Besides, he speaks to audiences large and small around the world and has done thousands of radio and television appearances. So he didn't reach his goals, but he didn't exactly come up with that fistful of mud either.

All those small steps he took at night and on weekends over the years immeasurably enhanced his joy in life and his economic freedom. By striving over the long haul for the big goals in life, even if you fall a little short, you are still way ahead of the game. When it comes to career management, think of stepping-stones and calendars. *You have everything to gain and nothing to lose by making the effort.*

Calendars Not Clocks

You live in a world that encourages you to demand instant gratification: "Have it all and have it now; life is tough and you are special; our product will make you somebody better instantly; you deserve it; you owe it to yourself; be someone better; be more attractive; be more popular, right now!" as the aptly named boob-tube tells you every eight minutes for five hours every day of your life.

> **How should I manage my life/my career differently?** Stay involved. Don't expect you have made it or that this world now owes you. Stay active in your associations. **Help** others at all times: to network, to grow and to learn.
>
> Nancy C. Anton, CPC. Talent Consultant, CIGNA. 20 years' experience.

This constant din of consumerism pulls your attention away from working toward a meaningful life for yourself. It encourages you to indulge in fantasies, living up to your income rather than living up your dreams. The result, all too often, is that you get in over your head, and, trapped like a mouse on a paddle wheel, you are too busy running in place to ever think about how you can make the dreams of your life come true.

Why not invest your time and energy in making your life unfold in ways that are meaningful to you? Take your dreams and turn them into concrete goals, by identifying the stepping-stones that will bring them to life. Then take those stepping-stones and in the spaces between each one, identify the smaller action-steps you'll take to carry you forward to the next stepping stone.

Then break each of those steps down into smaller actions, until there is always some small step you can take today; some small action that you can take toward a life goal, every day of your life. A step that once taken brings you a little closer to making one of your dreams a reality. What does this require? It requires applying the *critical think-ing* and *multitasking* skills that play such an important role in the success of your *core career* in another context.

Now that you've worked through *Secrets & Strategies,* you have everything you need to take control of your job search, your career, and your life; control of your destiny really is within your grasp. Lots of books tell you to pursue your dreams; this one tells you exactly how to make them a reality. Why not take the *transferable skills* and *professional values*—which you use to make your job more secure and your career more successful—and apply them to the pursuit of your life goals? Use the tools you have in your hands to bring your dreams to life.

So, if you wake up on the right side of the grass tomorrow morning, what will you do for the rest of your life? Will you watch your life slide by on a TV screen, or will you make it shine? It's your life, and it's your choice.

APPENDIX

THE EXPERT DATABASE

Name	**Wendy Adams**
Title	Founder
Company	The Career Coach
Specialization	Career Coaching, Career Transitions
Accreditations	CA, CCM, GCDF
Experience	20 years
Contact	*coachcompass@aol.com*
Website	*www.coachcompass.com/faqs.php*

Name	**Nancy C. Anton**
Title	Talent Consultant/ Recruiter
Company	CIGNA
Accreditations	Certified Personnel Consultant (CPC)
Experience	20 years
Contact	*Nanlife@gmail.com*
Website	*www.cigna.com/*

Name	**Marjean Bean**
Title	President
Company	Medit Staff, LLC
Specialization	Information Technology
Accreditations	Certified Personnel Consultant (CPC)
Experience	30+ years
Contact	*mbean@meditstaff.com*
Website	*www.meditstaff.com*

Name	**Alesia Benedict**
Title	Chief Executive Officer, GetInterviews.com
Company	GetInterviews.com
Specialization	Resumes, cover letters, social media job search, online profiles, interviewing guidance
Accreditations	Certified Professional Resume Writer (CPRW), Certified Job and Career Transition Coach (JCTC)
Experience	20+ years
Website	*www.getinterviews.com*

Name	**Jay Block**
Title	Author, President of The Jay Block Companies
Company	The Jay Block Companies
Specialization	Employment and Workplace Strategist and Author
Experience	20+ years
Contact	*jayblock@jayblock.com*
Website	*www.jayblock.com*

Name	**Jim Bright**
Title	Partner
Company	Bright & Associates
Specialization	Career Development, Coaching, Training, Writing, Speaking
Accreditations	BA (Hons) Psychology, PhD Psychology, Fellow Australian Psychological Society, Fellow Career Development Association Australia, Member National Career Development Association
Experience	22 years
Contact	*jim@brightandassociates.com.au*
Website	*www.brightandassociates.com.au*

Name	**Glenna Cose Brin**
Title	President
Company	Alliance Staff
Specialization	High-end administrative and mid-level financial placement generalist; Milwaukee focused; primarily in legal, health care administration, financial industries
Accreditations	Certified Personnel Consultant (CPC)
Experience	30+ years
Contact	*glenna@alliancestaff.com*
Website	*www.alliancestaff.com*

Name	**Joseph Camarda**
Title	President
Company	CAM Search and Consulting
Specialization	Human Resources, Accounting and Finance, and Health Care
Experience	25 years
Contact	*camsearch@aol.com*
Website	*www.linkedin.com/pub/joseph-j-camarda/a/a5/770*

Name	**Paul Cameron**
Title	President and Sr. Technology Recruiter
Company	DriveStaff, Inc.
Specialization	Technology professionals for Direct Hire and Contract Staffing
Experience	14 years
Contact	*paul@drivestaff.com*
Website	*www.drivestaff.com/*

Name	**Maynard G. Charron**
Title	President
Company	Paper Industry Recruitment (PIR)
Specialization	Management
Experience	30+ years
Contact	*mc@pirecruitment.com*
Website	*www.pirecruitment.com*

Name	**Allison Farber Cheston**
Title	Principal
Company	Allison Cheston & Associates, LLC
Specialization	Career Advisor to Mid-Career Executives and Young Adults
Accreditations	MA International Education, Certificate in Adult Career Planning (both NYU)
Experience	28 years
Contact	*Allison@allisoncheston.com*
Website	*www.allisoncheston.com*

Name	**Marsha Connolly**
Title	Managing Partner
Company	The New River Group
Specialization	Executive Coaching, Career Management, Professional Identity Management
	Advanced Certified Executive Coach, Marshall Goldsmith
	Certified Executive Coach, NCHL and GE Institute for Transformational Leadership
Experience	30 years
Contact	*marsha.connolly@thenewrivergroup.com*
Website	*www.thenewrivergroup.com*

Name	**Grant Cooper**
Title	Certified Resume Writer / President
Company	Strategic Resumes / Careerpro of New Orleans
Specialization	Professional and Executive Resumes
Accreditations	Certified Advanced Resume Writer (CARW)
Experience	17 years
Contact	*grant@resupro.com*
Website	*www.strategicresumes.com*

Name	**Al Daum**
Title	President
Company	Alan N. Daum & Associates, Inc.
Specialization	Process Automation Engineering
Accreditations	Certified Personnel Consultant (CPC)
Experience	36 years
Contact	*alan@adaum.com*
Website	*www.adaum.com*

Name	**Rich Gold**
Title	Senior Recruiter
Company	Smith Arnold Partners
Specialization	Finance
Accreditations	Certified Personnel Consultant (CPC)
Experience	20 years
Contact	*rgold@smitharnold.com*
Website	*www.smitharnold.com*

Name	**Meg Guiseppi**
Title	The C-level Executive Job Search Coach
Company	Executive Career Brand
Specialization	Executive Branding, Resume, Career Biography, LinkedIn Profiles, Online Identity Building, and Social Media Training
Accreditations	Reach Certified Personal Branding Strategist (CPBS), Reach Certified Online Identity Strategist (COIS), Certified 360Reach Brand Assessment Analyst, Master Resume Writer (MRW), Certified Professional Resume Writer (CPRW), Certified Employment Interview Consultant (CEIC), Certified VisualCV Creator
Experience	20+ years
Contact	*meg@executivecareerbrand.com*
Website	*www.executivecareerbrand.com*

Name	**Michelle Hagans**
Title	Recruiter
Company	Anu Resources Unlimited
Specialization	IT and Medical
Experience	20+ years
Contact	*mhagans@anuresources.com*
Website	*www.anuresources.com*

Name	**Rick Kean**
Title	Consultant, Retired
Company	A. M. Hamilton, Inc.
Specialization	Staffing and Staffing Training
Accreditations	BA Economics, Denison University; Graduate Study in Journalism, University of Missouri; Certified Personnel Consultant (CPC)
Experience	30+ years
Contact	*rickkean@amhinc.com*
Website	*www.amhinc.com*

Name	**Sean Koppelman**
Title	President
Company	The Talent Magnet
Specialization	Advertising, beauty, and entertainment
Experience	16 years
Contact	*sean@thetalentmagnet.com*
Website	*www.thetalentmagnet.com*

Name	**Eric Kramer**
Title	Chief Innovation Officer
Company	Innovative Career Services
Specialization	Career Coaching/Interview Training
Accreditations	Licensed Psychologist
Experience	10 years
Contact	*epkramer@gmail.com*
Website	*www.myinnovativecareer.com/about.php*

Name	**Janice Litvin**
Title	Executive Search Consultant
Company	Micro Search
Specialization	High-tech, Marketing
Accreditations	BS Math, U. of Texas Austin
Experience	20 years
Contact	*JLitvin@MicroSearchSF.com*
Website	*www.microsearchsf.com*

Name	**Rob Lockard**
Title	HR Manager
Company	The Centech Group, Inc.
Specialization	Human Resources
Accreditations	Senior Professional in Human Resources (SPHR)
Experience	9 years
Contact	*rob.lockard.sphr@gmail.com*
Website	*www.centechgroup.com*

Name	**Valentino Martinez**
Title	President
Company	V B Martinez Group, Inc.
Specialization	Recruitment and University Relations—Motivational Speaker on Getting and Keeping Careers on Track in the Twenty-First Century
Experience	38 years
Contact	*vbmartinezgroup@accessus.net*
Website	*www.managementconsultants.us.gy/40354/function.mysql-query*

Name	**Karen McGrath**
Title	Talent Acquisition Manager
Company	Enterprise Rent-A-Car
Accreditations	PHR
Experience	22 years
Contact	*karen.mcgrath@erac.com*
Website	*www.linkedin.com/in/karenmcgrath*

Name	**John T. Mooney**
Title	Human Capital Exec in transition
Company	J. Mooney dba Consultive Source
Specialization	Professional Development Practitioner and ICF Certified Coach
Experience	20+ years
Contact	*Jmooneyhr@aol.com*
Website	*www.linkedin.com/in/johnmooney*

Name	**Bob Morris**
Title	Recruiter/owner
Company	Storage Placements
Specialization	Filling revenue generating positions at data storage vendors
Experience	44 years
Contact	*bob@storageplacements.com*
Website	*www.storageplacements.com*

Name	**Joseph S. Murawski**
Title	Senior Recruiting Project Manager/ Executive Search Consultant
Company	Focused Hire
Specialization	Aerospace, Defense and High-Tech Electronics
Accreditations	Certified Personnel Consultant (CPC)
Experience	15 years
Contact	*Joe@focusedhire.com*
Website	*www.focusedhire.com*

Name	**Perry Newman**
Title	Executive Resume Writer/Career Coach
Company	Perry Newman CPC/CSMS
Specialization	Resume writing and career coaching for executives and middle level managers
Accreditations	Certified Personnel Consultant (CPC)
Experience	25 years
Contact	*perry@perrynewman.com*
Website	*www.perrynewman.com*

Name	**Olga Ocon**
Title	Executive Recruiter
Company	Busch International
Specialization	Focused in VP- and CEO-level searches in high-technology
Experience	15 years
Contact	*olga@buschint.com*
Website	*www.buschint.com/buschint.com/HOME.html*

Name	**George T. Olmstead**
Title	Managing Partner
Company	Olmstead Lynch & Kreutz
Specialization	Senior Management Recruiting; Senior Financial Searches
Experience	30 years
Contact	*george@olksearch.com*
Website	*www.olksearch.com*

Name	**Don Orlando**
Title	Owner
Company	The McLean Group
Specialization	Rising, senior, and very senior executives
Accreditations	Master's of Business Administration (MBA, Auburn University at Montgomery), Certified Professional Resume Writer (CPRW), Certified Job and Career Transition Coach (JCTC), Credentialed Career Master (CCM), Certified Career Management Coach (CCMC)
Experience	17 years
Contact	*dorlando@yourexecutivecareercoach.com*
Website	*www.mcleanllc.com*
Name	**Jim Rohan**
Title	Senior Partner
Company	J P Canon Associates
Specialization	Supply Chain Management
Experience	25 years
Contact	*jim@jpcanon.com*
Website	*www.jpcanon.com*
Name	**Faith Sheaffer-Polen**
Title	Senior Career Coach
Company	CareerCurve, LLC
Specialization	Executive coaching, career management, resume writing, adult learning and development, industrial/organizational psychology
Accreditations	Certified Career Management Coach, MS Industrial/ Organizational Psychology, pending conferral May, 2011
Experience	15 years
Contact	*fpolen@gmail.com*
Website	*www.careercurve.com*

Name	**Nancy Schuman**
Title	Vice President Marketing
Company	Lloyd Staffing
Specialization	Administration, Finance, Diversity, Sales, Supply Chain and IT
Accreditations	Certified Safety Professional (CSP)
Experience	30 years
Contact	nschuman@lloydstaffing.com
Website	www.lloydstaffing.com

Name	**Lisa Chenofsky Singer**
Title	Executive and Career Management Coach
Company	Chenofsky Singer & Associates
Specialization	Career Management and Conflict Resolution
Accreditations	Certified Executive Coach, International Coaching Federation member
Experience	20+ years
Contact	lchenofsky@gmail.com
Website	www.chenofskysinger.com

Name	**Mike Squires**
Title	Senior Technical Recruiter
Company	PayPal, an eBay Company
Specialization	Senior Technical Recruitment
Experience	15 years
Contact	mikesquires2@gmail.com
Website	www.linkedin.com/in/mikesquiresstaffing

Name	**Dean Swett**
Title	President
Company	Paramour Group, LLC
Specialization	Talent Representation
Experience	26 years
Contact	*dean@paramourgroup.com*
Website	*www.paramourgroup.com*

Name	**Bob Waldo**
Title	Principal Consultant
Company	Best Hire Consulting Services, LLC
Specialization	Candidate assessment and selection
Experience	20 years
Contact	*bob.waldo.recruiter@gmail.com*
Website	*www.hireconsultant.com*

Name	**Ron Weisinger**
Title	Principal Development
Company	LINKS Consulting
Specialization	Human Resources
Experience	20 years
Contact	*ronweisinger@comcast.net*
Website	*www.linkedin.com/in/ronweisinger*

Name	**Bill Wilhelm**
Title	Executive Recruiter
Company	Wilhelm and Associates, Inc.
Specialization	Industrial Sales and manufacturing management
Accreditations	Certified Personnel Consultant (CPC)
Experience	38 years
Contact	*wilh46@bellsouth.net*
Website	*www.linkedin.com/pub/bill-wilhelm/2/78a/3b5*

Name	**Denise Wilkerson**
Title	Director, Executive Search
Company	Global Edge Recruiting
Specialization	Medical Device, Biotechnology, Pharmaceuticals-Sales Marketing, Management
Accreditations	Registered Nurse (RN), Certified Personnel Consultant (CPC), Master of Human Resources Development (MHRD), Bachelor of Science in Nursing (BSN)
Experience	14+ years
Contact	*denise@globaledgerecruiting.com*
Website	*www.globaledgerecruiting.com*

Name	**Christine Wunderlin**
Title	Career Coach
Company	Christine Wunderlin Consulting
Specialization	Career Development
Accreditations	Master's Degree Counseling and Career Development; Certified Job and Career Transition Coach—Certification by the Career Planning and Adult Development Network, San Diego, CA
Experience	30+ years
Contact	*christinewunderlin@hotmail.com*
Website	*www.christinewunderlin.com*

INDEX

Adams, Wendy, 35, 204
Alan N. Daum & Associates, Inc., 46, 122, 208
Alliance Staff, 100, 142, 206
Allison Cheston & Associates, LLC, 207
Alumni associations, 51, 63, 187
A. M. Hamilton, Inc., 1, 18, 140, 168, 209
Anton, Nancy C., 8, 25, 58, 71, 94, 101, 112, 125, 163, 167, 176, 201, 204
Anu Resources Unlimited, 12, 22, 33, 60, 86, 105, 156, 169, 209
Anxiety and fear, 84–85, 131
ASCII format, 62
Associations
    alumni, 51, 63, 187
    civic, social, and spiritual, 56
    professional, 43, 49–51, 63, 177–78, 187

Baby boomers, 43, 45, 182
Bean, Marjean, 11, 23, 119, 132, 143, 204
Behavioral interview strategies, 108, 109–10
Behavioral profiles, 30–31, 87, 88
Benedict, Alesia, 147, 205
Benefits, 142, 160–61
Best Hire Consulting Services, LLC, 149, 216
Block, Jay, 8, 205
Body language, 12, 95–96
Boss, relationship with, 172–74, 179
Bright, Jim, 51, 136, 205
Bright & Associates, 51, 136, 205
Brin, Glenna Cose, 100, 142, 206
Busch International, 49, 85, 170, 213

Camarda, Joseph, 206
Cameron, Paul, 39, 68, 92, 206
CAM Search and Consulting, 206
CareerBuilder.com, 43
Career change, 183–89. See also Job changes, interview questions on
    case history, 198–200
    degree and, 192–93

networking and, 187–88
    overcoming obstacles to, 185–88
    perils of, 184–85
Career choice, 189–93
The Career Coach, 35, 204
CareerCurve, LLC, 67, 214
CAREER CZAR, 5
Career/job success, 165–202
    behavioral profiles for, 30–31, 87
    belief in oneself and, 170–71
    building blocks of, 193–95
    employability boosting strategies, 171–76
    experts on, 8, 112, 136, 137, 142
    as a marathon vs. a sprint, 4, 197
    starting small in, 167–69
    stepping-stones and calendars in, 197–202
THE CENTECH GROUP, Inc., 211
Chaos Theory of Careers (Bright), 51, 136
Charron, Maynard G., 104, 183, 207
Chenofsky Singer, Lisa, 3, 215
Chenofsky Singer & Associates, 3, 215
Cheston, Allison Farber, 53, 175, 189, 207
Christine Wunderlin Consulting, 5, 217
CIGNA, 8, 25, 58, 71, 94, 101, 112, 125, 163, 167, 176, 201, 204
Civic and social associations, 56
Commitment, 18, 19, 177, 183, 197, 198
Communication skills, 9, 15, 16, 122, 123, 137, 198, 200
    failure of, 167
    overview, 11–12
Company websites, 43, 88, 89
Connolly, Marsha, 137, 156, 166, 193, 198, 207
Consultive Source, 212
Conversations, 67–85. See also Telephone conversations
    capturing information in, 72
    with dream employers, 72–73
    etiquette in, 112
    initiating with hiring managers, 74–76
    live leads from dead ends, 82–84

painting a word-picture, 76–82
to quadruple chances of an interview, 73–74
techniques for, 111
tools for finding names for, 70–72
who to approach for, 68–69
Cooper, Grant, 151, 171, 185, 208
Core career, 3, 182, 183, 184, 197, 200, 202
desire and reality, 193–94
dream/entrepreneurial career leading from, 195–96
practicality of choice, 189–92
Core competencies
building, 171–72
resume section, 33–34, 35, 107
Corporate alumni associations, 51
Corporate culture, 159
Cover letters, 38–39, 73
Creativity, 15–17, 198
Critical thinking skills, 15, 16, 99, 122, 123, 127, 131, 132, 135, 137, 139, 140, 202
overview, 10–11
Criticism, interview questions on, 125–26

Daum, Al, 46, 122, 208
Deadlines, interview questions on, 122
Decision making, interview questions on, 125, 133, 137, 139
Degree, college, 192–93
Determination, 18, 198
DevelopmentLINKS Consulting, 9, 79, 107, 161, 166, 216
Digital dirt, 48
Dream career, 3, 182, 191, 193, 194, 195–97, 200, 201–2
Dream employers, 72–73
Dress and grooming, 12, 91–94, 166
DriveStaff, Inc., 39, 68, 92, 206
DWIs, interview questions on, 128

Economy
national, 5, 45, 75, 182, 189
personal, 19
Emotional intelligence, 7, 12, 102
Emotional maturity, 102, 127, 139–40
Employment agencies, 63
Employment contracts, 161–63
Encyclopedia of Associations, 51
Enlightened self-interest, 19, 170–71, 177, 182, 196
Enterprise Rent-A-Car, 21, 90, 106, 131, 139, 145, 179, 181, 211
Entrepreneurial career, 3, 182, 191, 193, 194–96, 197, 200

Ethics, 18
Etiquette, conversational, 112
Executive Briefings, 38–39
Executive Career Brand, 33, 54, 60, 65, 72, 110, 188, 209
Experience, interview questions on, 140–41, 147
Experienced interviewers, 103, 104–5
Eye contact, 96

Facebook.com, 17, 36, 44, 47, 48, 49, 62
Failure
attitude causing, 140
behavioral profiles for, 31, 88
Fair Credit and Reporting Act, 127
Family and friends, networking with, 54–56
Felonies, interview questions on, 128
Financial difficulties, interview questions on, 127–28
Financial security, building, 193
Firings, interview questions on, 120. *See also* Layoffs
First impressions, 95–96, 165–67
Focused Hire, 112, 212
Follow-up to interviews, 143–51

Gaps
in employment, 118, 121
in skills, 179, 186
Generations X and Y, 45
GetInterviews.com, 147, 205
Global Edge Recruiting, 17, 36, 62, 91, 117, 144, 217
Goals
falling short of, 200–202
importance of, 196–97
interview questions on, 132
starting toward now, 4–5
thinking about, 2–4
Gold, Rich, 90, 128, 208
Google, 61, 63, 70
Google News, 71, 89, 118
Guiseppi, Meg, 33, 54, 60, 65, 72, 110, 188, 209

Hagans, Michelle, 12, 22, 33, 60, 86, 105, 156, 169, 209
Handshake, 95
Headhunters, 48, 61–64, 75, 153, 190. *See also* Recruiters, corporate
Hidden job market, 42, 64–66, 71, 72
High-value job titles, 53, 64–65, 68–69, 72, 186, 189

Hiring managers
    initiating conversations with, 74–76
    tools for finding names of, 70–72
Hobbies and special interests, 56

Income, broadening sources of, 3
Inner circle, 176–78, 199
Innovative Career Services, 210
Intelligent enthusiasm, 100–102, 108, 143, 146
Internet. *See also* Company websites; Job sites; Social networking sites
    establishing a web presence, 53, 54
    filling out applications on, 60
    technical proficiency on, 10
Interview questions
    examples of, 115–42
    information-gathering, 113–14
    interviewee, 90, 94, 104, 108, 141–42
    listening to, 119
    requesting clarification on, 111
    for unconscious incompetents, 104
Interviews, 86–151. *See also* Interview questions
    anxiety during, 131
    conversation etiquette, 112
    conversation techniques, 111
    dress and grooming for, 91–94
    experienced interviewers, 103, 104–5
    first impressions in, 95–96
    five secrets to acing, 97–102
    follow-up to, 143–51
    interviewer peeves, 125, 139
    kit for, 89–91
    organization of, 103–8
    preparing for, 86–96
    quadrupling chances of obtaining, 73–74
    strategies in, 108–10
    talking too much in, 112, 116
    unconscious incompetent interviewers, 103, 104
In the Driver's Seat: Work-Life Skills for Young Adults (Cheston), 53, 175, 189
Inventions, assignment of, 162

The Jay Block Companies, 8, 205
Job changes, interview questions on, 118–19. *See also* Career change
Job interviews. *See* Interviews
Job offers. *See also* Negotiations
    accepting, 163
    declining, 151
    written confirmation of, 149, 161

Job search. *See* Conversations; Headhunters; Interviews; Job sites; Networking; Network-integrated job search; Research; Resume banks; Resumes
Job search networks, 56
Job security, 5, 171–76, 189, 194
Job sites, 5, 43, 45, 59–61
J P Canon Associates, 22, 90, 116, 134, 148, 214

Kean, Rick, 1, 18, 140, 168, 209
Keywords, 23–25, 34, 35, 48
Knock 'em Dead: Breaking into Management (Yate), 180
Knock 'em Dead: Professional Communication (Yate), 180
Knock 'em Dead: The Ultimate Job Search Guide (Yate), 20, 58, 66, 82, 85, 114, 121, 142, 164
Knockemdead.com, 20, 27, 32, 37, 40, 58, 59, 62, 63, 66, 70, 85, 142, 151, 164, 180, 185, 192
Knock 'em Dead Cover Letters (Yate), 40, 85
Knock 'em Dead Resumes (Yate), 40
Koppelman, Sean, 83, 93, 100, 155, 178, 191, 210
Kramer, Eric, 99, 210

Layoffs, 1. *See also* Firings, interview questions on
Leadership skills, 14–15, 16, 137
Letters/e-mails
    cover, 38–39, 73
    follow-up, 145–50
    job offer acceptance, 163
    job search, 39–40, 73, 142
    resignation, 163
    templates, 40, 142, 164
    thank-you, 144
LinkedIn.com, 36, 44, 47–49, 53, 62, 67, 170
Listening skills, 11
Little House on the Prairie (Wilder), 196
Litvin, Janice, 48, 210
Lloyd Staffing, 40, 43, 48, 69, 127, 128, 215
Lockard, Rob, 172, 186, 211

Manageability, 102, 138
Martinez, Valentino, 161, 163, 199, 211
McGrath, Karen, 21, 90, 106, 131, 139, 145, 179, 181, 211
The McLean Group, 36, 98, 214

Medit Staff, LLC, 11, 23, 119, 132, 143, 204
Mentors, 174–75, 179, 199
Micro Search, 48, 210
Mills, Jackie, 44
Monster.com, 43
Mooney, John T., 212
Morris, Bob, 119, 157, 167, 212
Motivation and energy, 17, 100–102
Multitasking skills, 9, 15, 16, 122, 123, 129, 132, 134, 140, 186, 200, 202
    overview, 12–13
Murawski, Joseph S., 112, 212

Names
    first *vs.* formal, 145–46
    hiring managers', finding, 70–72
Negotiations, 152–64
    on benefits, 160–61
    employment contracts and, 161–63
    job evaluation and, 157–60
    on salary, 152–56, 161
Networking, 46–58
    career change and, 187–88
    through job search networks, 56
    mindset, 57–58
    personal/community, 47, 54–56
    professional, 47–54
Network-integrated job search, 41–45
Newman, Perry, 4, 14, 42, 71, 109, 169, 177, 194, 213
The New River Group, 137, 156, 166, 193, 198, 207
Non-compete clauses, 162
Non-disclosure clauses, 162
Note taking, 144, 167

Ocon, Olga, 49, 85, 170, 213
Office Angels, 44
Olmstead, George T., 154, 190, 213
Olmstead Lynch & Kreutz, 154, 190, 213
Organizational abilities, 12–13, 15, 122, 140, 200
Orlando, Don, 36, 98, 214

Paper Industry Recruitment (PIR), 104, 183, 207
Paramour Group, LLC, 216
PayPal, 41, 64, 70, 88, 215
Performance Profile (resume section), 33, 35, 77–78, 81, 107, 117
Perry Newman CPC/CSMS, 213
Personal/community networking, 47, 54–56
Personal space, 95

Plan, Do, Review Cycle, 13, 122
Pride and integrity, 18
Problems (anticipating, preventing, and solving), 6, 10, 29, 87, 107, 115, 122, 123, 185–86, 188
    importance of, 99–100
    interview questions on, 124
Productivity, 5, 19
Professional associations, 43, 49–51, 63, 177–78, 187
Professional networking, 47–54
Professional persona, 7, 19, 86, 88, 101, 184
Professional values, 6, 8, 9–10, 15, 17–20, 87, 97, 100, 101, 113, 115, 121, 124, 130, 149, 150, 175, 177, 186, 188, 202
    in core/dream/entrepreneurial careers, 195–96
    defined, 9
    review of types, 17–19
    TJD and, 32
Promotions, 42
    changing jobs to obtain, 26–27
    how to pursue and win, 178–80
    missing out on, 171, 179
The Proteus Solution (Block), 8

Questions
    categories leading to job openings, 84
    interview (see Interview questions)
    for job evaluation, 157–60

Recruiters, corporate, 44, 48, 62–64, 69, 188. See also Headhunters
Recruitment process, 41–44
References, 52–53, 90, 121
Rejection, interview questions on, 139
Reliability, 18
Relocation packages, 162–63
Reposted jobs, 149
Research
    on the company, 86, 88–89, 117–18
    direct, 64–66, 189
    resources, 65–66
Resignations
    interview questions on, 121
    letters of, 163
Resume banks, 61–62
Resumes, 21–37, 47–48, 188
    becoming your, 86–88
    databases for, 21–22, 23–24, 34
    example of, 37
    familiarity with, 90
    important elements of, 22–25
    at interviews, 89, 106–7
    length of, 35

Resumes—*continued*
  naming docs, 40
  for promotions, 179, 180
  for recruiters, 62
  sending directly to manager, 73, 74
  six rules for building great, 32–37
  walking through, 106–7
Retirement, considering, 182–83
Rohan, Jim, 22, 90, 116, 134, 148, 214

Salary
  interview questions on, avoiding, 142
  negotiating, 152–56, 161
  on resumes, not, 35
Salary.com, 153
Sales jobs, interviews for, 139
Schuman, Nancy, 40, 43, 48, 69, 127, 128, 215
Secrets & Strategies (website section), 58, 70, 193
Severance agreements, 162
Sheaffer-Polen, Faith, 67, 214
Situational interview strategies, 108, 110
Six degrees of Kevin Bacon, 70
Skill development, 179, 186, 198–99
Small companies, 45
Small talk, 96
Smiling, 96, 100, 116
Smith Arnold Partners, 90, 128, 208
Social graces, 12
Social networking sites, 36, 43, 44, 53, 62, 63, 89, 187
  digital dirt on, 48
  effective use of, 47–49
Spiritual associations, 56
Squires, Mike, 41, 64, 70, 88, 215
Standard and Poor's (S & P), 66
Storage Placements, 119, 157, 167, 212
Strategic Resumes/Careerpro of New Orleans, 151, 171, 185, 208
Stress interview strategies, 108, 109
Swett, Dean, 216
Systems and procedures, 19–20, 125, 132, 133, 135

The Talent Magnet, 83, 93, 100, 155, 178, 191, 210
Target Job Deconstruction (TJD), 25–32, 48, 52, 77, 87, 88, 99, 115, 117, 126, 131, 136, 138, 139, 149, 152, 178
  career change and, 186, 188
  payoff at interviews, 107
  sequence, 26–32

Target job titles, 22–23, 24, 32, 35, 63
Teamwork skills, 15, 16, 44, 102, 122, 124, 131, 132, 137, 138, 169, 198
  overview, 13–14
Technical skills, 6, 15, 16, 87, 97–98, 107, 113, 121, 122, 123, 130, 135, 137, 138, 175, 176, 177, 186, 188, 198, 199, 200
  defined, 8
  improving, 171
  overview, 10
  problems caused by lack of, 127
Technology communication skills, 11
Telephone conversations
  dealing with fear of, 84–85
  interview follow-up, 148, 149, 150–51
  job search, 71–72, 73, 74–85
Thank-you letters, 144
Time management, 12–13, 15, 122, 134, 200
Titles. *See* High-value job titles; Target job titles
TJD. *See* Target Job Deconstruction
Transferable skills, 6, 9–17, 19–20, 87, 97, 98, 100, 102, 107, 113, 115, 121, 122, 123, 126, 130, 137, 138, 150, 152, 175, 177, 186, 188, 202
  in core/dream/entrepreneurial careers, 195–96
  defined, 8
  review of types, 10–17
  TJD and, 32
Twitter, 44

Unconscious incompetent interviewers, 103, 104

Vacuum Theory, 175–76
V B Martinez Group, Inc., 161, 163, 199, 211
Verbal skills, 11

Waldo, Bob, 149, 216
Websites. *See* Internet
Weisinger, Ron, 9, 79, 107, 161, 166, 216
Wikipedia.com, 49
Wilder, Laura Ingalls, 196
Wilhelm, Bill, 116, 165, 217
Wilhelm and Associates, Inc., 116, 165, 217
Wilkerson, Denise, 17, 36, 62, 91, 117, 144, 217
Writing skills, 11
Wunderlin, Christine, 5, 217